The Mustard Book

The Mustard Book

Written and Illustrated by

Jan Roberts-Dominguez

Macmillan Publishing Company   *New York*
Maxwell Macmillan Canada   *Toronto*
Maxwell Macmillan International   *New York Oxford Singapore Sydney*

*To Steve: partner, friend, and husband. You make
it happen. You make me laugh. You make it all
worthwhile.*

Copyright text and illustrations © 1993 by Jan Roberts-Dominguez

Macmillan Publishing Company   Maxwell Macmillan Canada, Inc.
866 Third Avenue   1200 Eglinton Avenue East, Suite 200
New York, NY 10022   Don Mills, Ontario M3C 3N1

Macmillan Publishing Company is part of the Maxwell Communication
Group of Companies.

Library of Congress Cataloging-in-Publication Data
Roberts-Dominguez, Jan.
The mustard book / Jan Roberts-Dominguez.
p.   cm.
ISBN 0-02-603641-X
1. Cookery (Mustard)   2. Mustard (Condiment)   I. Title.
TX819.M87R63   1993
641.8'384—dc20   93-19559   CIP

Macmillan books are available at special discounts for bulk purchases for
sales promotions, premiums, fund-raising, or educational use. For details, contact:

Special Sales Director, Macmillan Publishing Company
866 Third Avenue, New York, NY 10022

10 9 8 7 6 5 4 3 2 1

Printed in the United States of America

Acknowledgments

There are many people who had a hand in this book. And to all of them I give a hearty Thank You.

First, to my agent, Jane Dystel, for her canny vision that turned an idea into a proposal which became a project. Her energy, enthusiasm, and sense of timing are remarkable. Thank goodness she's on my side!

A special thanks to my parents, Margaret and Will Roberts, for their unflagging support, research, and steady flow of good ideas, not to mention iron-clad palates throughout the mustard-tasting phase.

To my editor, Pam Hoenig; it was truly a pleasure working with such a kind yet relentlessly thorough soul. And to Pam's assistant, Justin Schwartz, for helping all of us through "the delivery," but even before that, for being one of the most valued members of my cross-country taste panel.

To Elise Marton, for her gracious, insightful copy editing.

To design director, Anne Scatto, and designer Laura Hough, for an elegant book.

To Oregon's own condiment king, Gene Biggi of Beavertown Foods, for his technical expertise and willingness to pass along a few secrets of the trade.

To Barry Levenson, founder and curator of The Mount Horeb Mustard Museum in Mount Horeb, Wisconsin, for the information, networking, and wonderful tidbits of mustard trivia he provided through his conversations and newsletter, *The Proper Mustard*.

In Corvallis, to Jennifer Lorenz at Country Notions Gift Gallery, and to Deege and Doug Squires of the Happy Cooker, for the generous loan of their lovely china, linens, and all the other accouterments I needed to create the still-life sets for my watercolors.

For general inspiration, thanks to friend and food preserver Chris Rossi.

And finally, to my husband, Steve, who stood before our open refrigerator on far too many nights with the same lament, "There's nothing in here but mustard!"—thanks for the hours and hours of time you devoted to the manuscript and repair of my creative spirit, on an empty stomach yet.

Let's eat.

Contents

Introduction

We'd been in Paris less than four hours and were wandering along the Left Bank when hunger struck. Although a traditional French bistro was high on our itinerary, my friends and I agreed that the sausage vendor's cart less than ten yards away had lunch written all over it. The delicious aroma wafting its way noseward was irresistible.

After tucking the plump and juicy sausages into steamy-hot and crusty rolls, the vendor waggled her fingers between two mustard pots.

"Spicy or no?" she asked.

"Spicy!" we said in unison, and she slathered our picnic fare with a deep golden condiment flecked with tiny yellow and brown mustard seeds.

We crossed the road to the river and settled ourselves on top of a huge stone wall, the Seine passing just twenty feet below our dangling Nikes. There, with Paris all around, I took my first bite of my first French meal—and vowed that when I returned to the States I would track down this fantastic mustard and stock vast amounts of it in my refrigerator.

Well, not only did I become an avid buyer of the varied styles and types of mustard, I also learned how to produce those zesty wonders in my own kitchen. But why, you ask, write a book on the subject? Perhaps you haven't been to a supermarket lately. Or a winery gift shop. Or a holiday boutique. Novel mustards of all styles, colors, and flavors, from "apricot" to "Zinfandel," are shouldering their way onto the shelves. And whenever I pass along my own latest mustard creations in a newspaper column, the response is just overwhelming. It seems that everyone wants to get in on the act. You see, there's something truly satisfying about taming the fiery character of the mustard seeds and then using it to elevate the mundane, be it a hot dog or a salad dressing, to the sublime.

Interpretation of what this far-flung condiment should be, and how it should be integrated into the local cuisine, varies from place to place around the world. Above all else, *The Mustard Book* is a celebration of this marvelous diversity. So each recipe, though newly created, reflects the character of a particular culinary philosophy. It may do so in a traditional way, or it may be a more personalized rendition. But it will always deliver a sense of the exotic, and of something distinctly different.

As a matter of fact, the ease with which mustards can be used to satisfy that endless human craving for new taste sensations may complete the explanation for their appeal. Unless, that is, you throw in the instant-gratification factor. You see, as simple as mustards are to concoct, there is still enough leeway for creativity to make every cook feel special. If you have a particularly fine collection of Spanish sherries, then sherry will be the liquid of choice. Visualize, if you will, lightly steamed green beans draped with a sherry mustard-tinged cream sauce. French tarragon is thriving in your herb garden? Then why not devise your very own version of tarragon Dijon? Your overflow of the summer's sun-dried tomatoes will blend into a rich and rosy California mustard. Laced with flecks of oregano and garlic, it's the perfect complement to a garden sandwich of sliced avocado, smoked turkey, salami, and mixed greens.

This is power cooking at its finest: you, a batch of mustard seeds, and virtually no boundaries, adding up to some of the most flexible condiments imaginable. Use them to thicken a sauce in nanoseconds. Add instant flavor to a stir-fry. Impart roughness (whole grain) or smoothness (cream style) of texture to a sauce. Delight a friend with a gift of mustard. The prospect of opening pretty little jars that promise such extravagant taste sensations is indeed beguiling. The image of wholesomeness will also be appreciated. Designer mustards—redolent of natural ingredients like peppercorns, cumin, or pineapple—impart their passion without a lot of extra fat and calories.

In the end, I hope you will come to view this book as a source of inspiration to improvise, rather than just a collection of recipes. Take ideas from such novel food experiences as come your way. For example, the idea for a pickled olive mustard popped into my head as a natural progression from research I happened to do on the New Orleans muffulata sandwich. This was less a consequence of food knowledge than of being in the habit of asking myself, "Now, what else could I do with this great olive paste?" Remember, if serendipity came in a bottle, it would be labeled Mustard. Explore and enjoy!

Chapter One

The History of Mustard

You have to wonder what possessed that first person to take the fiery-hot mustard seed and turn it into a condiment. In the beginning, the seeds were used in various medicinal ways. But who came up with the idea of having the potent little poultice cross over into cuisine? Might some early chef with too many ladles in the wine crock have turned to his apprentice and said: "I have an idea, young Potsherd. Let's take some of that mustard plaster the Healer fixed up for your sore toe and feed it to the king. It'll take his head off. Wouldn't that be a hoot?" One can visualize a sobered chef, quaking before the victimized monarch the next day, only to be honored with the proclamation that henceforth meals were always to be accompanied by this amazing new concoction that so effectively disguised the rancidity of all-too-well-aged meat.

Well, it's just a theory. What we do know is that mustard was used in cooking long before the Egyptians were entombing their kings with bags of it for the afterlife. Apparently, people of that society were wont to chew the seeds with their meals because it did indeed mask the off flavors of degraded perishables that could not be wasted. Perhaps of more immediacy to us is that an entire century before Columbus set off for the new world, the French city of Dijon was already turning out its famous mustard by the barrelful. Also by that time, Pope John XXII—whose affinity for mustard was apparently intense—had granted his nephew the very first title of Premier Moutardier du Pape. That's Italian for "Mustard Maker to the Pope."

By the early 1600s storage and cooking styles had improved so dramatically that spices were no longer used primarily to make spoiled food more palatable. People were definitely hooked on the tantalizing zing provided by a hearty dose of mustard, and so its use as a condiment continued. For the rest of that century, various styles of ground mustard powder abounded.

Up to this point, however, the powders were noticeably rugged in texture, resulting in coarse-grained pastes. Then, in 1720, an English-woman by the name of Mrs. Clements developed a commercially useful method for separating the tough, fibrous outer coating of the seeds from the powder. Suddenly fine-textured mustards were *haute*.

But the new process didn't speed anything up. Until the middle of the nineteenth century, a single mustard maker couldn't manufacture more than about thirty-five pounds of the condiment per day. In France in 1853, Maurice Grey invented a machine that could crush, grind, and sieve the seeds in one speedy operation. This meant that production could be increased almost threefold. Grey was awarded great honors for his invention and became the first mustard maker whose product could be labeled with the prestigious phrase "By royal appointment."

Jumping ahead only a few years, mustard history was again made in 1866 when Grey joined forces with another mustard maker of the time, Auguste Poupon. Forevermore they would be known as Grey-Poupon. But of course.

Meanwhile, across the English Channel, one Jeremiah Colman had purchased a simple windmill so he could mill flour. Within a decade his business was going so well that in 1814 he bought out another mill, which was being used to mill mustard as well as flour. Colman took this new venture very seriously, examining every aspect of the business to guarantee the production of the best mustard powder he felt possible. By the mid-1800s he had perfected the process by which one of the most consistently excellent mustard powders on the market—even to this very day—is produced.

It's a well-guarded company secret, of course, but the general principles of Colman's mustard making have leaked into the public domain. What is known is that Colman's uses only specially selected brown and white seeds provided by English growers. As raw seeds arrive at the factory, they are examined, cleaned, dried, and stored. As needed, these seeds are ground and sifted separately. Then mustard powders are blended in a very specific ratio of white to brown and packed into the familiar yellow tins. It's this finicky attention to correct proportions, not to mention the quality of seeds and style of grinding, that guarantees a consistent product.

Americans, it seems, were slow to jump on the mustard bandwagon. Even as late as 1904, we were turning up our noses at the potent import. At the time, most manufacturers just assumed we weren't used to the pungency of the prevailing varieties. But Francis French ultimately had the insight to attribute lackluster sales to a collective picky palate. Folks, he believed, simply didn't like the basic flavor of the English and French mustards. So this president of the nation's largest mustard company, based in New Jersey, asked his plant superintendent, George Dunn, to come up with a new formula that was light and creamy, with a milder flavor. The resulting golden yellow condiment, marketed as French's Cream Salad Brand, was a hit. Within a couple of years, sales had topped a million dollars and the frankfurter had gained a never-to-be-spurned sidekick. So long as there are hot dogs to be eaten, Americans will not turn their backs on good old "Mellow Yellow."

And so, something that began as nothing more than a blend of tiny seeds and liquid has gone through staggering growth, particularly in recent years. With each nation interpreting what this spicy condiment should be, and how it should be integrated into the local cuisine, the world now has innumerable variations upon the zesty theme of mustard.

Now, industry giants around the world have had to make room for a growing number of smaller, independent mustard makers, creative mavericks concocting beguiling brews with such intriguing names as Blue Coyote Hot Pepper Mustard Relish and Mike's Magic Mustard. Classic Dijon styles are prominent—thanks to their worldwide appeal—but these days the small designer mustards, redolent of flavorings as diverse as peppercorns, cumin, and pineapple, are capturing a large share of the market.

Variations do abound in astounding numbers. At the Mount Horeb Mustard Museum in Wisconsin, for example, mustard aficionado Barry Levenson has amassed an ever-growing collection of more than 1,373 domestic and international varieties.

Is this recent popularity a fleeting thing? Or will history prove that mustard is going through a bona fide renaissance? With health-conscious and taste-conscious consumers growing in numbers, the logical conclusion is that mustard will only become more popular. Clearly, this condiment projects an image of elegant wholesomeness; from basic stone-ground to designer styles, it represents a creative way to add flavor without a lot of extra fat and calories.

Chapter Two

Getting Started

If your idea of making mustard has thus far consisted of stirring a little bit of water (or wine, or ale, or vinegar) into powdered mustard, then you're in for a pleasant surprise. Even if you've taken that concept a step or so further by adding a sprinkling of herbs or sugar or an egg yolk, you have yet to savor what a real homemade mustard can be. You see, I believe in starting with the whole seeds. It's the only way to achieve the purest, most balanced of mustard flavorings. Otherwise, you're relying on whatever powdered mustard blend you happen to have purchased. Even if it's Colman's—which most agree is the superior powdered mustard blend on the market these days—the flavors and textures you can create are limited. Granted, I have provided a few recipes that use mustard powder, but that's because I was reproducing a particular traditional preparation, such as a Japanese hot mustard or a Swedish dilled mustard.

All of my recipes in which whole mustard seeds are used follow the same basic steps:

Soak. First, you combine the seeds with a liquid and let the mixture sit for two days. This simple step—which is very similar to the process commercial mustard makers follow and is usually not found in recipes for homemade mustards—makes all the difference. By allowing the seeds time to absorb the liquid, to soften and plump, before pureeing them or adding other ingredients, you make the finished product creamier and more richly flavored. Depending on the dryness of the seeds—and believe me, it does vary—you'll notice that your seeds either lap up the liquid very quickly or slowly absorb it over the allotted time. It's something you have to monitor. Since the idea is to keep the seeds just barely covered with liquid, if you have a thirsty batch you'll have to add additional liquid at more frequent intervals, especially during the first twenty-four hours.

Blend. After the soak, the thoroughly plumped seeds and whatever liquid remains are transferred to a food processor so the mixture can be pureed to the desired consistency. At this point I must pause to stress that a food processor really is the necessary piece of equipment, not a blender. A food processor provides the proper blade action to thoroughly attack the tough outer coating of the seeds with a good deal of control; a blender simply is not as effective because it purees the mixture too quickly, taking the mustard beyond a coarse-grain consistency before you know it.

This is usually the point at which you add in any other ingredients, such as shallots, sun-dried tomatoes, fresh herbs, or garlic. You may be surprised at how long my recipes instruct you to run the food processor. Generally, you keep the seeds in motion for three to six minutes, which is a long time by most standards. But if you're patient and follow directions, you'll see the mixture transform before your eyes from one with defined seeds and liquid to a somewhat creamy and then very creamy paste. As the seeds' crisp hulls crack and break, the pulpy centers are thrown into solution, where they help thicken and flavor the mustard.

Press. If you're aiming for a velvety-smooth mustard rather than a mildly grainy or whole-grained mustard, then, as the final step, the paste will have to be forced through a sieve. In order to end up with a fine puree, you will need to use a fine sieve. Commercial mustard makers have no problem locating this type of equipment, but it's a different story for the home cook. The sieves and strainers sold in the average housewares store are fine for straining potatoes, green beans, or rice from boiling water, but the holes are much too large for mustard-making purposes. When you press the mustard through, most of the seeds or broken hulls pass right through as well. However, there is an easy-to-find utensil on the market that does work, even though it wasn't designed for this purpose. It's called a "splatter guard," because its true purpose in life is to rest on top of a frying pan during cooking and keep hot grease from spattering out of the pan and onto the stove. It resembles a round hand-held mirror, except that where the mirror would be there's a circle of fine-mesh metal. This screen is fine enough (about twenty holes per inch) to remove the hulls and seeds from the paste as it's pressed through with a rubber spatula. There are several brands on the market, but you may want to obtain your splatter guard from a shop that sells fine-quality cookware. You'll pay a little more, but I have found that the inexpensive brands sold in the cookware aisles of supermarkets aren't sturdy enough to stand up to the stress of the sieving operation for long.

The Mustard Seeds

Mustard gets its kick from three types of mustard seeds: black, brown, and white (commonly referred to as "yellow" since the seeds are actually a pale yellow color). The black ones come from black mustard, *Brassica nigra*; brown from *B. juncea*; pale brown or yellow seeds from white mustard, *Sinapis alba*. The black and brown seeds contribute the familiar "hot" or pungent flavor of mustard; the yellow mustard, although milder, also contributes its own character, a very distinctive mustard flavor.

For an interesting exercise that will clearly show the differences in the seeds' personalities flavorwise, place two or three of each kind in your mouth, one variety at a time, beginning with the yellow. Bite down on the seeds and mix the pieces around in your mouth to get them moist. You may be surprised to note that the yellow seeds exhibit no fire at all at this point, and almost no taste. But the flavor will develop over several minutes if you leave the seeds in your mouth long enough, and ultimately you will recognize the familiar "mustard" seasoning.

Now place two or three of the tiny brown seeds in your mouth. The fire won't immediately begin—it takes time. What you'll notice is that the brown seeds are decidedly mustier in flavor than the yellow. Once you progress to the black, the musty flavor will be even more pronounced, as will the spiciness and fire.

Commercially available mustard powder is a combination of yellow and black or brown mustard seeds. As for mustard preparations, there are countless styles on the market, from hot and highly seasoned to mild. The traditional Chinese mustard, usually prepared from dry mustard powder and water or flat beer, is near the hot end of the scale, whereas the all-American "prepared" mustard (based almost entirely on *Sinapis alba* seeds) and German whole-seed mustards are milder.

The Liquids

The ultimate pungency of a prepared mustard is achieved by mixing the mustard seeds or powder with cold water, which facilitates the enzymatic formation of the necessary essential oils. Acids, such as vinegar—and, to a lesser degree, wine or beer—produce a less favorable environment for the enzyme and, thus, a slightly tamer condiment. But remember, *slightly* is the operative word. These mustard preparations are still potent, even after the flavors have improved and mellowed during the two- to three-week aging process.

I like using vinegar in my recipes because I feel it helps to create a balance of flavors. When making your own mustards, remember that there is a plethora of vinegars available to you. Distilled and cider vinegars will provide the strongest flavors. Wine and fruit-flavored vinegars (such as raspberry) have a slightly milder impact; don't bother with expensive Champagne vinegars, because the flavor is much too subtle to justify the cost. Balsamic and malt vinegars provide a unique and distinctly sweet flavor. Rice vinegar is slightly sweet but very mild.

Other liquids traditionally used in making mustards are wine, beer, and a variety of hard liquors such as rum or whiskey. Since there is less acid in these products than there is in vinegar, the finished mustard will tend to be more robust in flavor. It's important to use liquor of decent quality, but it doesn't have to be expensive, since any subtleties in the liquid will be lost in the final preparation.

Besides taste, however, you have to keep the ultimate color you wish to achieve in mind. For instance, if you want a light, delicately colored mustard, don't start with balsamic, malt, or red wine vinegar, or a dark beer or red wine. Any of these ingredients will turn the mustard a rather dark and murky color.

When preparing a mustard, don't add a boiling-hot liquid; I've noticed that subjecting the seeds or powder to temperatures at or near the boiling point (212°F, at sea level) tends to make the final product rather bitter or, at the very least, flat. This carries through to the process of cooking with your mustards. The flavor tends to hold better when the mustard is added toward the end of cooking.

Storage and a Word on Food Safety

Many of the recipes in this book benefit from a few weeks of aging. Some need to rest for only a day or two in order to allow the flavors to mingle together a bit. At the end of each recipe I've provided aging recommendations, if appropriate.

Please store your mustards in the refrigerator. Although it's hard to imagine any bacterium with half a brain wanting to reproduce in such a fiery potion, food-safety experts caution that it is a possibility. As a result, it's best to store questionable batches in the refrigerator. Questionable, by my definition, is any recipe calling for liquids other than just vinegar. When this is the case, you should mark your labels "Keep refrigerated." Of course, most of these mustards will safely survive room temperature during the gift-giving phase. But putting your homemade mustards through an unrefrigerated cross-country trek via regular mail is not advisable. If you can bear the expense, pack them with dry ice in an insulated box and ship via an overnight parcel service.

Chapter Three

European Mustards

Because it's one of the easiest plants to grow, mustard has been cultivated and used throughout Europe for ages. Of course, the styles of mustard, the condiment, have always been as varied as the cuisines it is used in.

FRANCE

Dijon

Is any other single word as synonymous with mustard? Perhaps not, but mustards departing from the traditional Dijon style abound. On the table of any given bistro in Paris, for example, you can expect to find a generous selection of mustards in little pots in the center of your table, all begging to be slathered onto chunks of the ever-present French bread as you wait for your "real" meal to arrive.

For a French mustard to be labeled "Dijon," it must come from the Dijon region (which a large percentage do) and be made in the manner set forth by the French government. Mustards made outside of the Dijon region, but that still comply with the guidelines, are generally labeled "Dijon-style." These regulations were created in 1937, when the French government became actively involved in overseeing the production of mustard. The parameters of the edict include the type of seeds and

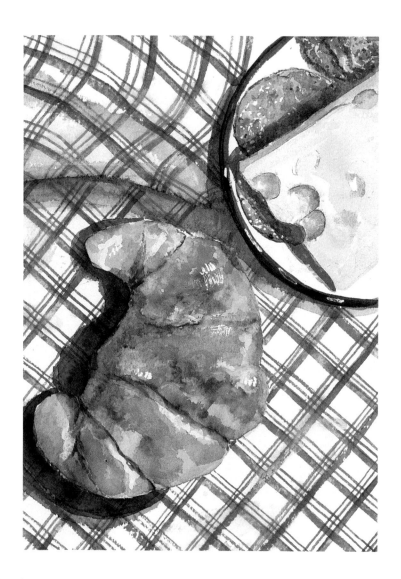

liquid to be used, as well as the method of preparation. As a result, to be called Dijon mustard, by French decree, it must contain only black and/or brown seeds—the use of yellow seeds is forbidden—and be blended only with verjuice (unfermented wine), wine, wine vinegar, or a combination thereof. Salt, spices, and water are acceptable, but aside from sulfur dioxide, which can be added to protect the color, nothing else is permitted if the mustard maker wishes to retain the coveted Dijon mustard label.

Even the grinding of the seeds is carefully monitored and has been elevated into a fine art. After only the best of seeds are selected, sorted, and soaked, they are sent to the mill, where they are gently ground with the seasonings and liquid of choice. The grinding is done with such fine precision that the brown husks are merely broken instead of crushed, so they can be easily removed. If not sifted from the mustard at this point, the husks would taint the rich amber color produced by the yellow kernel inside. Once the paste is made, it's aged for about eight days in oak casks.

Another popular French mustard is a whole-grained variety made in Bordeaux. It is milder than Dijon mustard, is darker in color since it contains the darker seed coats, and is made with red wine vinegar. It's also heavily seasoned with tarragon, sugar, and additional herbs and spices. Although many Dijon purists turn their noses up at this hearty condiment, it is considered a marvelous choice for fresh eating—particularly with sausages, ham, and sandwiches.

Classic Dijon

1¼ cups brown mustard seeds
1 cup mustard powder (this a
  necessary compromise, and fully
  endorsed by Mr. Biggi)
1 cup water
1 cup distilled vinegar
¼ cup dry white wine
7 cloves garlic, chopped
3 tablespoons white wine
  Worcestershire sauce
1 teaspoon ground allspice
1 teaspoon sugar
2¼ teaspoons salt
¼ teaspoon turmeric
¼ teaspoon ground white pepper
¼ teaspoon ground mace
⅛ teaspoon ground cinnamon

Without benefit of the special grinding equipment available to commercial mustard makers, the making of a true Dijon—according to French law—is not realistically possible in a home kitchen. So in order to come up with a mustard that looks and tastes as much like a classic Dijon as possible, I have had to fudge with the process and ingredients. If the French Mustard Police come and cart me away, so be it. My accessory in crime was Gene Biggi, president of Beaverton Foods in Beaverton, Oregon. Gene was helpful throughout this project. His company produces an extensive line of mustards, and Gene has a good nose for what makes a mustard work. He sampled my first attempt at a Dijon style (which we both felt was horrid) and offered a few suggestions on technique and ingredients. The biggest tip he provided was a suggestion that I find some way to put the mustard through a low-temperature heating. This, said Gene, would deactivate the potent enzyme lurking within brown mustard seeds but would not destroy the flavor. My mind flipped through all of the logical ways a home cook could easily apply long-term, low-level heat to a batch of mustard. The answer was sitting on an upper shelf in my girlfriend's garage: an electric slow-cooker. If you want to make my Classic Dijon but, like me, have long since disposed of this relic from the '60s, do what I did—borrow one. The results are worth the effort.

In a nonaluminum pot or jar, combine the mustard seeds, mustard powder, water, vinegar, and wine. Cover and soak for 48 hours, adding additional water, vinegar, and wine (in the correct proportions) if necessary to maintain enough liquid to cover the seeds. Since the mixture tends to separate into three distinct layers, stir it at least once a day.

Scrape the soaked seeds mixture into a food processor, add the garlic, and process until the mustard turns from liquid and seeds to a creamy mixture flecked with seeds. Let the food processor run a little longer than with other mustard recipes—5 or 6 minutes. Besides creating a particularly creamy mustard (that will still be somewhat grainy, of course), the warmth that builds up while the blades are turning will tame the harsh flavor of the mustard powder. Add additional water, vinegar, and wine (in correct proportions) as necessary to keep the mustard very creamy during the processing; keep in mind that it will thicken slightly upon standing.

Now for the taming-of-the-fire step which helps turn this into a truly classic Dijon-style mustard: Scrape the mustard into an electric slow-cooker. Cook on the "Low" setting, covered, for 4 hours. Stir the mixture about 3 times during the first hour, then whenever you think of it for the remaining time. You never want the mixture to reach a simmer—that's too hot and will create a bitter rather than smooth flavor—but to merely "stew" at about 130°F to 140°F. After the heat treatment, stir in the remaining ingredients. Press the mixture through a fine-mesh metal strainer.

I've found that this is a mustard that benefits greatly from at least 3 to 4 weeks of aging in the refrigerator. You will be surprised at how the flavors meld and mellow in the process.

Makes about 1¾ cups.

One final note: Since you've gone to so much work for a mere 1¾ cups of mustard, consider doubling the batch; you'll have room in the slow-cooker and will certainly find plenty to do with the extra mustard, as illustrated by the following variations.

Green peppercorn: After sieving, stir in 2 tablespoons of rinsed and coarsely chopped green peppercorns.

Tarragon: After sieving, stir in 3 tablespoons finely minced fresh tarragon leaves. (If fresh is unavailable, use 1 tablespoon dried, crumbled.)

Provençal: After sieving, stir in 1 tablespoon of dried *herbes de Provence* (mixed herbs), crumbled.

Garlic: When preparing the basic batch of Dijon, use 11 or 12 cloves of garlic instead of 7.

Shallot: Simmer ¾ cup minced shallots in ¼ cup dry white wine over medium heat until they are softened, about 5 to 7 minutes. Let the mixture cool, then stir into the basic batch after it has been pressed through the sieve, and puree the mixture in a blender or food processor one last time.

Citrus: After sieving, stir in 1 tablespoon finely grated orange, lemon, or lime zest.

Black olive: For a smooth-textured mustard, stir ¼ cup chopped canned olives into the basic batch after it has been pressed through the sieve, then puree the mixture in a blender or food processor one last time. For a coarser product, simply stir the olives into the batch of mustard after sieving and skip the final pureeing.

Sun-dried tomato: Stir ½ cup drained and coarsely chopped oil-packed sun-dried tomatoes into the basic batch after it has been pressed through the sieve, then puree in a blender or food processor one last time. The mustard will turn deep red and very thick. You may want to thin it slightly with additional wine and vinegar.

Pesto: After sieving, stir in ¼ cup commercially prepared or homemade pesto.

Roasted pepper: After sieving, stir in ¼ cup minced roasted (see note on page 127) and peeled peppers (it's your choice, but I recommend either a sweet red or green bell, or one of the mild green chile peppers, such as Anaheim or poblano). For a smoother texture, puree the mustard-pepper mixture.

⅔ cup yellow mustard seeds
½ cup brown mustard seeds
1 cup red wine vinegar
½ cup dry red wine, such as
    Cabernet Sauvignon, Pinot Noir,
    or Beaujolais (of course, if you
    want to be authentic, opt for a
    red Bordeaux, if your budget will
    allow the indulgence)
4 cloves garlic, minced
2 tablespoons sugar
2 tablespoons white wine
    Worcestershire sauce
2 teaspoons salt
½ teaspoon dried tarragon,
    crumbled
1 teaspoon dried marjoram,
    crumbled
1 teaspoon ground white pepper
1 teaspoon turmeric

Bordeaux Mustard

A whole-grained French mustard that's delicious with sausage. For a simple and flavorful sauce, whisk several spoonsful into a cup of heavy cream.

In a nonaluminum pot or jar, combine the mustard seeds, vinegar, wine, and garlic; cover and soak for 48 hours, adding additional vinegar and wine (in the correct proportions) if necessary to maintain enough liquid to cover the seeds.

Scrape the soaked seeds into a food processor. Add the remaining ingredients and process until the mustard turns from a liquid and seeds to a creamy mixture flecked with seeds. This takes 3 to 4 minutes, so be patient. Add additional vinegar as necessary to create a nice creamy mustard; keep in mind that it will thicken slightly upon standing. This mustard benefits from a week or two of aging.

Makes about 3¼ cups.

Salad of Baby Greens and Bunch Onions with Dijon Vinaigrette

A simple salad of fresh baby greens—or mesclun, as it's known in the French outdoor markets—and another early-summer specialty, bunch onions, which are simply young globe onions with the leaves attached. Dressed in a simple but well-executed vinaigrette, this is a delightful mixture.

Whisk together the vinegar, mustard, pepper, and a sprinkling of salt. Whisk in the olive oil, then adjust the seasonings. Toss enough of the dressing with the remaining salad ingredients to evenly coat everything.

Makes 6 to 8 servings.

⅓ cup red wine vinegar

2 tablespoons Dijon mustard (either the Classic or any of the flavored Dijons will work—see pages 20–24)

Salt and freshly ground black pepper to taste

⅔ cup extra virgin olive oil

2 quarts fresh mesclun (mixed baby greens)

2 or 3 bunch onions, sliced (using about ⅓ of the green part)

2 cups fresh vegetables, such as roasted (see note on page 127) red bell pepper, zucchini, scallions, and cucumber

Other leafy things, including fresh bits of basil, tarragon, chervil, thyme, sorrel, watercress, and young dandelion leaves

European Mustards

25

ITALY

The Medicis, who were the rulers of Florence through the mid- to late fifteenth century, were fond of mustard, but what they ate was not at all similar to modern mustard: It consisted of scraps of stale bread, crushed mustard seeds, and almonds, soaked together in water and vinegar, then passed through a sieve.

Although Italians have very little use for mustard as a condiment, they have made delectable use of mustard oil in their unique specialty known as mostarda. This special preparation originated in the city of Cremona and is more of a chutney than a mustard, since it combines a melange of preserved fruits—figs, plums, raisins, cherries, and apricots—with a sweet-tangy syrup containing mustard oil and garlic. It is usually served with mixed boiled meats as well as zampone, a sausage from Modena. If it sounds odd, consider the wonderful interplay of flavors when you combine pork with applesauce, mint jelly with lamb, and turkey with cranberry sauce.

Mostarda

As mentioned above, this is an Italian condiment best described as a dried-fruit and mustard chutney. Be sure to use only quality dried fruits, such as those available at well-stocked health food stores. Since mustard oil is such a difficult thing to obtain these days (unless you have an Indian food store in your neighborhood), I have adapted the recipe as follows.

In a nonaluminum pot or jar, combine the mustard seeds, mustard powder, ¾ cup of the vinegar, and the sherry; cover and soak for 48 hours, adding additional vinegar and sherry (in the correct proportions) if necessary to maintain enough liquid to cover the seeds.

In a medium-size saucepan, combine the remaining vinegar with the sugar. Bring to a boil and simmer, uncovered, for 5 minutes over medium heat. Remove from the heat and stir in the salt and dried fruits; let the mixture sit about 30 minutes so the raisins can plump and the other pieces of fruit can soften.

While the fruit mixture is cooling, scrape about half of the mustard mixture into a food processor or blender and process 3 or 4 minutes, just enough to create a relatively creamy mixture. Scrape this mustard, as well as the remaining whole soaked mustard seeds, into the pan with the fruit, stir well to combine, and adjust the seasonings, adding additional salt if necessary. If the mostarda gets too thick after cooling, add additional vinegar and sherry (in the correct proportions). Mostarda will keep for several months in the refrigerator.

Makes about 3¾ cups.

½ cup yellow mustard seeds
½ cup mustard powder
1¼ cups white wine vinegar
¾ cup dry sherry
1 cup sugar
2 teaspoons salt
½ cup firmly packed golden raisins
½ cup firmly packed finely chopped dried apricots
½ cup firmly packed finely chopped dried figs
¼ cup firmly packed finely chopped candied cherries
¼ cup firmly packed finely chopped candied orange peel

Pesto Mustard

½ cup yellow mustard seeds
¾ cup balsamic vinegar
¼ cup water
2 to 3 cloves garlic (it depends on how much garlic is in your pesto), chopped
1½ teaspoons salt
¼ cup store-bought or homemade pesto (recipe follows)

This mustard was inspired by a bountiful supply of basil in my garden. It came together quickly and became an instant hit among friends. Although not authentic, I picture it being used in the modern Italian kitchen whenever a recipe needs a subtle kick. It's particularly good added to a simple oil and vinegar dressing.

In a nonaluminum pot or jar, combine the mustard seeds, vinegar, water, and garlic; cover and soak for 48 hours, adding additional vinegar and water (in the correct proportions) if necessary to maintain enough liquid to cover the seeds.

Scrape the soaked seeds into a food processor. Add the salt and pesto and process until the mustard turns from liquid and seeds to a creamy mixture flecked with seeds. This takes 3 to 4 minutes. Add additional vinegar and water as necessary to create a nice creamy mustard; keep in mind that it will thicken slightly upon standing. This mustard can be used immediately.

Makes about 1⅔ cups.

Pesto

1 cup packed fresh basil leaves
2 cloves garlic, peeled
1 tablespoon chopped fresh parsley
2 tablespoons pine nuts
2 tablespoons freshly grated Parmesan cheese
¼ teaspoon salt
¼ cup olive oil

Combine the basil, garlic, and parsley in a blender and process until finely chopped. Add the pine nuts, Parmesan, and salt and process just until blended. With the machine running, slowly add the olive oil and process until a smooth paste is formed. Store up to two weeks in the refrigerator, or up to three months in the freezer.

Makes 1½ cups.

Roasted Garlic Mustard

You'd think that a mustard boasting thirty cloves of garlic would be a potent concoction. But roasting tames the garlic dragon, and aging several weeks seems to improve the flavor even more.

With a sharp knife or kitchen shears, trim away the pointed stem end from each head of garlic, exposing the bulbs but leaving them intact. Peel excess papery skin from each head, then place the heads in a small, deep-sided baking dish. Add the sherry and olive oil, cover the dish tightly, and bake in a preheated 225°F oven just until tender, 50 minutes to 1 hour (the time will vary depending on the size and age of the garlic). Remove from the oven and let the heads cool in the cooking liquid.

In a nonaluminum pot or jar, combine the mustard seeds and vinegar. Pour the cooking liquid from the baked garlic into a measuring cup and add enough additional sherry to bring the total volume to ½ cup. Add this to the mustard and vinegar; cover and let soak in the refrigerator for 48 hours, adding additional vinegar and sherry (in the correct proportions) if necessary to maintain enough liquid to cover the seeds.

Sometime while the seeds are soaking, finish the garlic preparation: Pry each bulb away from its head; to peel, snip the pointed tip with kitchen shears, make a slice along the flat side, then squeeze the bulb free from the peel. Refrigerate until ready to proceed with the recipe.

Scrape the soaked seeds into a food processor. Add the peeled, roasted garlic cloves and the salt, and process until the mustard turns from liquid and seeds to a creamy mixture flecked with seeds. This takes 3 to 4 minutes. Add additional vinegar and sherry (in the correct proportions)

3 heads (yes, heads, not bulbs!) garlic (about 30 cloves)
½ cup dry sherry, plus more as needed
2 tablespoons olive oil
⅔ cup yellow mustard seeds
¼ cup brown mustard seeds
1 cup cider vinegar
2 teaspoons salt

as necessary to create a nice creamy mustard; keep in mind that it will thicken slightly upon standing.

Makes about 3¼ cups.

White Beans and Scallions in Pesto Vinaigrette

A delicious and traditional tuna salad from Italy.

3 cups cooked white kidney beans (also known as cannellini beans), prepared as described below

3 scallions, both green and white parts, finely chopped

One 3-ounce can albacore tuna, well drained and gently flaked

¼ cup finely minced oil-packed sun-dried tomatoes, drained (reserve the oil for the vinaigrette)

Salt to taste

Pesto Vinaigrette (recipe follows)

Combine the beans, scallions, tuna, and sun-dried tomatoes in a medium-size bowl. Lightly salt the mixture and gently toss to combine. Drizzle on the vinaigrette and toss again to thoroughly coat the ingredients.

Makes 4 servings.

To cook the beans: Place 1½ cups of dried beans in a large bowl with 2 quarts of water. Cover and let stand at room temperature for at least 8 hours or overnight. (A quicker method is to combine the beans and water in a pot, bring the water to a boil, remove from the heat, and let stand at room temperature, covered, for 3 hours.) Drain the beans, then place in a pot with 4 cups of water for every cup of soaked beans. Bring the water to a boil over high heat, then reduce the heat to medium or medium-low and simmer, partially covered, until tender, about 1 to 1½ hours.

This makes 3 cups cooked beans.

Pesto Vinaigrette

In a small bowl, whisk together the vinegar, pesto mustard, pepper, and salt. Whisk in the olive oil. This will keep about 2 weeks in the refrigerator.

Makes about ¾ cup.

¼ cup white wine vinegar
1 tablespoon Pesto Mustard (see page 28)
¼ teaspoon ground white pepper
¼ teaspoon salt
½ cup extra virgin olive oil

Bruschetta

In a bowl, combine the ricotta cheese, shredded carrot, Parmesan cheese, scallions, parsley, garlic mustard, and basil. Cut the bread in half horizontally, then place the halves, cut side up, on a baking sheet. You may have to trim the loaf from the cut side to obtain halves that measure about 1 inch thick. You may also have to trim a bit off the crust bottoms so that the halves sit firmly on the baking sheet. Brush the cut surface of each half with olive oil, then broil until the surface is toasted to a deep golden-brown. Remove the bread from the oven and cut each half into two or three pieces (depending on how large a serving you want). Spread each piece with some of the ricotta/mistard mixture. Loosely pleat the slices of pastrami on top of the ricotta spread, then sprinkle on the mozzarella. Return the bread to the baking sheet and bake in a preheated 400°F oven until the mozzarella melts and the ricotta mixture has warmed, 7 to 10 minutes. Garnish each slice with more parsley, and pass additional mustard at the table.

Makes 4 to 6 servings

1 cup ricotta cheese
¼ cup shredded carrot
¼ cup freshly grated Parmesan cheese
3 tablespoons chopped scallions, both green and white parts
2 tablespoons minced fresh parsley, plus extra for garnish
2 tablespoons Roasted Garlic Mustard (see page 29)
1 tablespoon finely minced fresh basil or 1 teaspoon dried, crumbled
1 whole loaf crusty Italian or French bread
Olive oil (optional, but tasty!)
¾ pound deli-cut pastrami
1 cup shredded mozzarella cheese

Mesquite~Broiled Chicken, Gruyère, and Sun~Dried Tomato Salad

3 boneless chicken breast halves, skinned

4 ounces Black Forest ham (available at German delicatessens and at the deli counters of large supermarkets), julienne-cut to measure 1 cup

1½ cups grated Gruyère cheese

1 medium-size red bell pepper, roasted (see note on page 127), peeled, seeded, and cut into strips

½ cup oil-packed sun-dried tomatoes, drained (reserve oil for dressing) and diced

1 to 2 tablespoons drained, rinsed, and coarsely chopped capers

Sunny Vinaigrette (recipe follows)

Mixed greens (1 head romaine lettuce combined with some green-leaf lettuce and perhaps some arugula or escarole if it's available), torn into bite-size pieces

Pesto Mayonnaise (see note)

There are a lot of wonderful things going on in this salad: dynamite flavor combinations, lively color and texture, and, if artfully arranged, an elegant presentation.

Grill the chicken over mesquite coals, if available (otherwise, over regular charcoal briquettes); chill until cool enough to handle. This may be done up to 24 hours ahead; refrigerate until ready to use.

Dice the chicken breasts into ¼- to ½-inch pieces. In a large bowl, combine the cut-up chicken, ham, 1 cup of the cheese, the bell pepper, sun-dried tomatoes, and capers. Toss with the vinaigrette until all the ingredients are well coated; chill for at least 30 minutes to blend the flavors. This can be done 2 or 3 hours ahead.

When ready to serve, arrange the greens on individual plates. Distribute the chicken mixture evenly among the plates, arranging it attractively on top of the bed of greens; garnish with a sprinkling of the remaining Gruyère. The pesto mayonnaise can be served on the side (in individual ramekins), or you can place a dollop of it on each serving and pass the rest.

Makes 4 entrée or 6 first-course salads.

Note: To make pesto mayonnaise, combine 4 parts mayonnaise and 1 part pesto. For 6 servings, mix ½ cup fine-quality store-bought mayonnaise with 2 tablespoons store-bought or homemade pesto (see page 28). It will keep in the refrigerator for up to 1 week.

Sunny Vinaigrette

In a small bowl, combine the lemon juice, salt, pesto mustard, pepper, and Worcestershire sauce. Blend well with a wire whisk. Continue whisking as you slowly add the olive oil. Adjust the seasonings. Can be made up to 2 or 3 days ahead, covered, and stored in the refrigerator. **Makes about ⅔ cup.**

Note: Be sure to use the olive oil that was packed with the sun-dried tomatoes (see previous recipe); the flavor is wonderful and blends beautifully with the salad.

2 tablespoons fresh lemon juice
½ teaspoon salt
2 to 3 teaspoons Pesto Mustard (see page 28)
Freshly ground black pepper to taste
Several dashes of Worcestershire sauce
½ cup olive oil (see note)

Fennel and Lentil Soup

Fennel is a remarkable vegetable. In its raw state the flavor is overwhelmingly that of anise. But with a bit of heat and time on the burner, it mellows to a delicate, slightly sweet character with a hint of celery. A bit of herbed mustard gives just the right amount of thickening and unique flavor to this soup.

Place the chicken broth and thighs in a large pot over high heat. Bring to a boil, then reduce the heat to medium, cover, and simmer for 15 minutes. Add the lentils, fennel, onion, and garlic and continue cooking until the lentils are just tender (do not let them get too mushy), about 30 minutes. Remove from the heat. Remove the chicken thighs from the soup and pull the meat off the bones, leaving it in at least 1-inch chunks; discard the bones. Put the meat back in the soup, add the

6 cups canned or homemade chicken broth
4 chicken thighs, skinned
1 cup dried lentils, picked over, rinsed, and drained
1½ cups chopped fennel bulb (about half a bulb)
1 cup chopped onion
2 cloves garlic, minced or pressed
1 cup diced canned tomatoes
4½ teaspoons mustard (one of the herbed varieties from this chapter, such as the Pesto Mustard—page 28—or the Classic Dijon variations—page 20)

tomatoes, whisk in the mustard, then bring to a boil just to reheat the mixture before serving. To round out the meal, serve with a tossed green salad and hot corn bread.

Makes 2 quarts; 6 servings.

Scallop, Mushroom, and Caper Sauté over Focaccia Bread

1 round brown-and-serve focaccia
  bread
1 to 2 tablespoons olive oil
Freshly grated Parmesan cheese
3 tablespoons butter
3 cups sliced mushrooms
2 cups sliced celery
1½ cups chopped onion
¼ teaspoon dillweed
¼ teaspoon salt
¼ teaspoon ground white pepper
2 tablespoons anisette (see note on
  page 35)
2 tablespoons drained and rinsed
  capers
¾ pound bay scallops, rinsed and
  drained (this removes any "fishi-
  ness" from frozen scallops)
1⅔ cups light cream or half-and-
  half
2 to 2½ teaspoons Roasted Garlic
  Mustard (see page 29)

You should be able to find focaccia bread tucked in among the other baked goods on your supermarket's bread aisle. Otherwise, stop by your favorite Italian deli.

Place the focaccia bread on a baking sheet, brush with the olive oil, and sprinkle liberally with Parmesan cheese. Bake in a preheated 400°F oven until golden, about 20 minutes. Keep warm until ready to serve.

Meanwhile, melt the butter in a large skillet, then add the mushrooms, celery, and onion and cook, stirring, over medium heat until the onion is soft and the mushrooms have released their liquid, about 5 minutes. Add the dill weed, salt, pepper, anisette, and capers and continue cooking until the liquid is almost evaporated. Add the scallops and continue cooking until they become opaque, about 3 minutes. Add the cream and cook until it reduces by about half and the mixture thickens, about 5 minutes. Stir in the mustard, then adjust the flavoring.

To serve, cut 4 wedges from the hot loaf of focaccia bread (don't feel you have to use the entire loaf; gauge the size of the wedge by the size of the diner!). Spoon on a portion of the scallop mixture and serve.

Makes 4 servings.

Note: Anisette is an essential ingredient in this recipe. The faint licorice flavor is a delicious complement to scallops. However, if you happen to have Pernod in your liquor cabinet, this could also be used (begin with 3 tablespoons, adding more to taste). About ½ cup of finely chopped fresh fennel bulb also works; just sauté along with the vegetables.

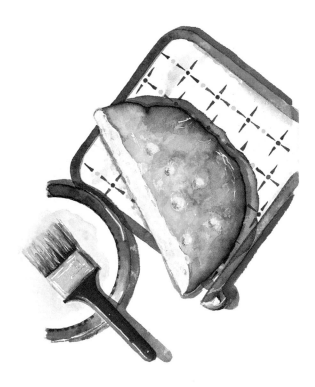

SPAIN

With its lush Mediterranean climate, Spain can boast of a generous harvest. Indeed, the earthy flavors of fresh tomatoes, olive oil, garlic, peppers, onions, nuts, raisins, and herbs are deeply rooted in the Spanish soul. And then there are the world-class sherries, as well as local and imported spices.

Mustard was introduced to Spain by the Caliphs around 800 A.D., when the region was under Arab occupation. As in Italy, traditional Spanish cuisine does not make wide use of mustard as a condiment, at least not to the degree of German, French, and even British cuisines. However, as the world shrinks and foods and cultures from neighboring countries cross borders, it doesn't take much of an imagination to visualize the kinds of mustards that would find their way into a Spaniard's kitchen.

Muffulata Mustard

The inspiration for this mustard comes from New Orleans, where the muffulata sandwich—a hearty concoction of Italian-style meats and cheeses, slathered with a rich olive and garlic relish—was created decades ago. It seemed to me that the zesty, full-flavored olive relish would make a delicious mustard and would combine well with the sunny flavors of Spain, since olives, olive oils, and garlic are such integral parts of Spanish cuisine. Muffulata mustard combines particularly well with some of the popular Spanish bar fare known as tapas, which is why this mustard has ended up in this particular section of the book.

In a nonaluminum pot or jar, combine the mustard seeds and vinegar; cover and soak for 48 hours, adding additional vinegar if necessary to maintain enough liquid to cover the seeds.

Below are two options for completing this mustard. My preference is for the textured version, in which the seeds are left whole, because I feel the flavors are more vivid and the visual impact lovelier.

For a textured mustard (one with tender-yet-whole mustard seeds mingling with the zesty-flavored olive relish): Simply combine the soaked seeds with the relish and salt.

For a smoother-style mustard: Scrape the soaked seeds into a food processor; add the relish and salt and process until the mixture turns from liquid and seeds to a creamy mixture flecked with seeds and bits of olive. The process takes at least 3 to 4 minutes. You may need to add additional balsamic vinegar as necessary to create a nice creamy mustard; keep in mind that it will thicken slightly upon standing. This is a mustard that can be enjoyed immediately.

Makes about 3½ cups.

¾ cup yellow mustard seeds
1 cup balsamic vinegar
1 cup Muffulata Olive Relish
  (recipe follows)
2 teaspoons salt

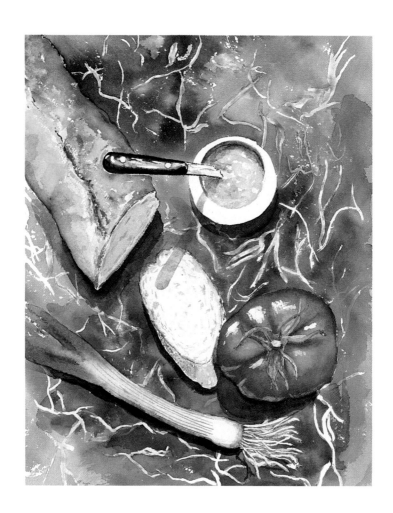

Muffulata Olive Relish

This is the marvelous concoction I use to make the Muffulata Mustard. However, it's a wonderful mixture in its own right. Place it in a bowl alongside slices of a crusty baguette for a simple appetizer; spread it on a poor-boy sandwich that you've piled high with a selection of sliced meats, cheeses, tomato, and pickled peppers.

Place the olives, onion, parsley, vinegar, garlic, capers, oregano, and pepper in a food processor. Pulse the mixture until the ingredients are finely chopped. Add the olive oil and continue processing until the mixture is thoroughly chopped but not pureed. This will keep in the refrigerator for at least 2 weeks.

Makes 1 cup.

½ cup coarsely chopped pimiento-stuffed olives
½ cup coarsely chopped pitted black olives
¼ cup chopped red onion
¼ cup minced fresh parsley
2 tablespoons balsamic vinegar
1 tablespoon minced garlic
1 teaspoon drained and rinsed capers
¼ teaspoon dried oregano, crumbled
¼ teaspoon freshly ground black pepper
⅓ cup extra virgin olive oil

Green Peppercorn and Sherry Mustard

In a nonaluminum pot or jar, combine the mustard seeds, vinegar, sherry, and peppercorns; cover and soak for 48 hours, adding additional vinegar and sherry (in the correct proportions) if necessary to maintain enough liquid to cover the seeds.

Scrape the soaked seeds into a food processor; add the olive oil and salt and process until the mixture turns from liquid and seeds to a creamy mixture flecked with seeds and bits of peppercorn. The process takes at least 3 to 4 minutes. You may need to add additional balsamic vinegar as necessary to create a nice creamy mustard; keep in mind that it will thicken slightly upon standing. Give this mustard at least two weeks to fully develop in flavor.

Makes about 2 cups.

½ cup yellow mustard seeds
¼ cup brown mustard seeds
¾ cup balsamic vinegar
½ cup dry sherry
2 tablespoons rinsed and drained green peppercorns
⅓ cup olive oil
2 teaspoons salt

Herbed Mustard with Balsamic Vinegar

¼ cup yellow mustard seeds
1 cup balsamic vinegar
3 tablespoons finely chopped fresh basil or 1 tablespoon dried, crumbled
1 tablespoon finely minced fresh oregano or 1 teaspoon dried, crumbled
1 tablespoon honey
2 teaspoons salt

Aceto balsamico, or balsamic vinegar, is a mellow, reddish brown Italian vinegar, typically from Modena, that's made from sweet wine. The good ones undergo a long aging process (measured in years, not months or weeks), and one pays dearly for the wait.

In a nonaluminum pot or jar, combine the mustard seeds and vinegar; cover and soak for 48 hours, adding additional vinegar if necessary to maintain enough liquid to cover the seeds.

Scrape the soaked seeds into a food processor; add the basil, oregano, honey, and salt and process until the mixture turns from liquid and seeds to a creamy mixture flecked with seeds. The process takes at least 3 to 4 minutes, so be patient. You may need to add additional balsamic vinegar as necessary to create a nice creamy mustard; keep in mind that it will thicken slightly upon standing. This mustard seems to benefit from a week or two of aging.

Makes 2 cups.

Cream Sherry Mustard with Toasted Almonds and Hazelnuts

For a rich flavor, toast the nuts to a deep golden hue.

In a nonaluminum pot or jar, combine the mustard seeds, vinegar, sherry, and garlic; cover and soak for 48 hours, adding additional vinegar and sherry (in the correct proportions) if necessary to maintain enough liquid to cover the seeds.

Scrape the soaked seeds into a food processor. Add the almonds, hazelnuts, and salt and process until the mustard becomes fairly creamy but still contains quite a few whole mustard seeds. This will take no more than 2 or 3 minutes. Add additional vinegar and sherry (in the correct proportions) as necessary to create the desired consistency; keep in mind that it will thicken slightly upon standing. No aging is required.

Makes 2¼ scant cups.

Note: To toast the nuts, place them on an ungreased baking sheet in a preheated 300°F oven and bake until lightly browned. While the nuts are still warm, rub them between your hands or in a towel to remove the skins.

1 cup yellow mustard seeds
¼ cup balsamic vinegar
¼ cup cream sherry
1 clove garlic, chopped
½ cup almonds, toasted (see note below) and coarsely chopped
½ cup hazelnuts, toasted (see note below) and coarsely chopped
2 teaspoons salt

Chorizo Empanadas

2 tablespoons olive oil

1 large yellow onion, diced

¼ pound mushrooms, finely chopped

3 cloves garlic, minced

¾ pound Italian sausage, casings removed and meat crumbled into very small chunks

2 teaspoons dried thyme, crumbled

1 teaspoon dried oregano, crumbled

¼ teaspoon red pepper flakes

¼ teaspoon ground cayenne pepper

¼ teaspoon ground white pepper

½ cup tomato paste

¼ cup dry sherry

Salt to taste

Empanada dough (recipe follows), divided and rolled into 16 rounds

1 large egg, lightly beaten

Mustard and Olive Oil Sauce for dipping (see page 46)

The empanada is Spain's answer to the portable meat pie. Although it is a flavorful treat in its own right, the creamy mustard and olive oil sauce that I have created is a delectable accompaniment.

In a large saucepan, heat the olive oil over medium heat. Add the onion, mushrooms, and garlic and cook, stirring, until the onion is lightly golden and the mushrooms' liquid has been released and evaporated. Add the sausage and continue cooking over medium to medium-high heat until it has browned on all sides. Drain off as much fat as possible, then stir in the thyme, oregano, peppers, tomato paste, and sherry. Bring the mixture to a gentle boil, then reduce the heat and simmer over medium-low heat until quite thick. Add the salt and adjust the seasonings; let the mixture cool to room temperature. (This filling may be prepared up to 2 days ahead. When ready to assemble, bring it to room temperature.)

Place about 2 rounded tablespoons of the filling on one side of each circle of dough, leaving a border of about ¼ inch. Gently fold the dough over on top of the filling, forming a half moon. Be sure to press the edges firmly together. Then, for an additional seal and to create a decorative border, beginning at one end, roll and press the seam edge toward the filling. The edge will look like a twisted rope.

Place the empanadas on an ungreased baking sheet, brush the tops gently with the beaten egg, and bake in a preheated 400°F oven until golden brown, about 25 minutes. Serve immediately, chilled, or at room temperature, accompanied by the sauce.

Makes 16 empanadas.

European Mustards

Empanada Dough

2 cups all-purpose flour
½ teaspoon salt
1 cup (2 sticks) chilled butter, cut
    into 16 chunks
4 to 6 tablespoons cold water

Combine the flour and salt, then cut in the butter using a pastry blender or two knives until the mixture resembles coarse cornmeal. Add the water 1 tablespoon at a time, tossing and mixing, until the dough holds together.

Form the dough into a ball, cover with plastic wrap, and refrigerate for 1 hour. Divide the dough into 4 equal portions, then divide each portion into 4 equal chunks. Cover the divided dough with a damp cloth and let it rest at room temperature for 15 minutes. Form each portion of dough into a ball. Roll each ball into a 3-inch-wide circle.

Makes 16 empanadas.

Mustard and Olive Oil Sauce

¼ cup Cream Sherry Mustard with
    Toasted Almonds and Hazelnuts
    (see page 43)
¼ cup extra virgin olive oil (see
    note below)

Whisk together the mustard and olive oil, and use as a dipping sauce for the empanadas. This also makes a tasty sauce for steamed vegetables, or a dip for cooked artichokes.

Makes ½ cup.

Note: If you can obtain the garlic-flavored olive oil made by Boyajian's (see Sources at the back of the book), this would be a marvelous place to use it.

Fava Beans in Casserole with Tomatoes

Of all the beans you're likely to encounter in the marketplace each spring or early summer, the fava is probably the least understood, at least in the United States. But favas are a popular bean throughout Spain. They also happen to be one of my favorites. A fresh-from-the-field fava has a brilliant green color when cooked, mild flavor, and a tender, slightly starchy character. If you can't find the fabulous fava in your area, it's perfectly acceptable to substitute frozen lima beans.

This simple casserole has a very Mediterranean flavor to it, thanks to the fresh oregano, olive oil, and tomato. It makes a wonderful winter side dish to roast lamb, chicken, or pot roast.

After shelling, blanch the beans in a large pot of rapidly boiling water for 4 minutes to loosen their outer skins. Drain the beans and plunge them into cold water, then drain again. Slip off the outer bean skins. Combine the skinned beans with the tomatoes and their juice, onion, olive oil, mustard, garlic, oregano, and salt. The mixture will be very soupy at this point. Pour it into a shallow, lightly greased 2½- to 3-quart baking dish. Generously sprinkle the top of the casserole with pepper. The casserole may be refrigerated for several hours at this point.

Bake in a preheated 400°F oven until the mixture becomes very thick and the top has browned nicely, 45 minutes to 1 hour. Serve hot or at room temperature.

Makes 8 servings.

3 cups shelled fava beans (3 to 4 pounds of unshelled beans)

Three 14½-ounce cans peeled and diced tomatoes, chopped

1 large onion, chopped

¼ cup olive oil

2 tablespoons Muffulata Mustard (see page 36), Green Peppercorn and Sherry Mustard (page 41), or other fine-quality herbed mustard

2 cloves garlic, minced

1 tablespoon chopped fresh oregano or 1 teaspoon dried, crumbled

1 teaspoon salt

Freshly ground black pepper to taste

Pa Amb Tomaquet

1 large, crusty loaf sourdough
French bread, cut into ½-inch-
thick slices
About 8 cloves garlic
Very ripe tomatoes, halved crosswise
Extra virgin olive oil
Herbed Mustard with Balsamic
Vinegar (see page 42)
Scallions, both green and white
parts, coarsely chopped

With a name that means "bread with tomato," these popular tapas are a celebration of the basics: the fine-quality bread, robust tomatoes, and luscious olive oils of this beautiful country.

Toast the bread on both sides to a rich golden brown; set aside in a 150°F oven to keep warm.

Peel each clove of garlic, halve it lengthwise, and arrange on a platter alongside the tomato halves (one tomato half per person). In a small bowl whisk together equal parts olive oil and mustard.

To serve, set out the toasted bread on a platter alongside the tomato halves and garlic, the bowl of mustard-olive oil sauce, and a dish of chopped scallions. Diners rub a garlic clove on the bread, then rub and squeeze the cut side of a tomato half on the bread, pressing so that the juice, seeds, and a bit of pulp spread onto the bread. Finally, diners drizzle on a bit of the sauce, sprinkle with scallions, and enjoy, straight out of hand—with the juicy pulp of the tomato still dripping down their fingers. Messy, but so delicious that as long as you're among friends, who cares?

Fennel Sautéed with Garlic in Mustard Cream Sauce

Like the fava bean, fennel is another vegetable that is still more popular in Spain, Italy, and France than in the United States. But we're catching up.

Wash and trim the fennel bulbs. Slice into rounds, then coarsely chop. Melt the butter in a medium-size pan over medium heat. Add the fennel and cook, stirring, until tender, about 5 minutes. Add the garlic and continue cooking another 2 or 3 minutes. Stir in the cream, sherry, and mustard and simmer until the cream is reduced and the sauce is thickened. Season with salt, then sprinkle with the Parmesan cheese and pass under the broiler for a few moments to brown the top. (If your saucepan does not have a heatproof handle, either cover the handle with aluminum foil or transfer the mixture to a shallow gratin dish before broiling.)

Makes 4 servings.

2 *pounds fennel bulbs with 1 inch of the stalks*
2 *tablespoons butter, margarine, or olive oil*
1 *clove garlic, chopped*
⅓ *cup light cream or half-and-half*
3 *tablespoons dry sherry*
2 *teaspoons Green Peppercorn and Sherry Mustard (see page 41)*
Salt to taste
⅓ *cup freshly grated Parmesan cheese*

The Mustard Book

50

SCANDINAVIA

By the end of April, Scandinavian days are long and sunny. From April into September, the foods are fresh and light, much like the season, and include healthful offerings from the garden—berries, lettuces, and a plethora of vegetables—as well as bounty from the sea.

The fresh herbs of spring, particularly dill, have always found their way into the Scandinavian kitchen, to be sprinkled into the sauces and mustards of the house. In Denmark a cook is apt to boil an evening meal of goose in clear, fresh water with a little thyme, then serve it up in moist, thick slices with sharp, sweet dilled mustard on the side. When a Scandinavian dish requires an assertive note, a sweet-sour mustard is almost always a part of the solution, be it a mustard-dill sauce atop gravlax, the traditional delicacy of salmon cured with sugar, salt, and dill, or a thin sheet of mustard on an open-faced sandwich.

Swedish Mustard

This hot, smooth, and sweet mustard is particularly good with baked ham or smoked pork.

Place all the ingredients in a food processor and process until well blended, about 2 minutes, stopping halfway through to scrape down the sides. Scrape into a container and refrigerate at least 24 hours before using.

Makes about 1 cup.

¾ cup mustard powder
¼ cup firmly packed light brown sugar
¼ cup cider vinegar
2 tablespoons boiling water
2 tablespoons vegetable oil
1 tablespoon Worcestershire sauce
1 teaspoon salt

Dilled Mustard

¾ cup yellow mustard seeds
½ cup mustard powder
1½ cups cider vinegar
½ cup water
2 tablespoons sugar
3 tablespoons minced fresh dill or
  1 tablespoon dried, crumbled
2 teaspoons salt

In a nonaluminum pot or jar, combine the mustard seeds, mustard powder, vinegar, and water; cover and soak for 48 hours, adding additional vinegar and water (in the correct proportions) if necessary to maintain enough liquid to cover the seeds.

Scrape the soaked seeds mixture into a food processor. Add the sugar, dill, and salt and process until the mustard turns from liquid and seeds to a creamy mixture flecked with seeds. Let the food processor run a little longer than with the other mustard recipes—5 or 6 minutes. Besides creating a particularly creamy mustard, the warmth that builds up while the blades are turning will tame the harsh flavor of the mustard powder. Add additional vinegar and water (in the correct proportions) as necessary to keep the mustard very creamy during the processing; keep in mind that it will thicken slightly upon standing. This mustard can be used right away, but it improves in flavor after 2 or 3 weeks in the refrigerator.

Makes about 3¼ cups.

Fresh Herb and Shallot Mustard

½ cup yellow mustard seeds
¼ cup brown mustard seeds
1 cup cider vinegar
1 cup dry white wine
1 cup finely chopped shallots
1 tablespoon minced fresh tarragon
or 1 teaspoon dried, crumbled
1 tablespoon minced fresh rosemary
or 1 teaspoon dried, crumbled
1½ teaspoons salt

For a stronger onion flavor, yellow onions can stand in for the shallots.

In a nonaluminum pot or jar, combine the mustard seeds and vinegar; cover and soak for 48 hours, adding additional vinegar if necessary to maintain enough liquid to cover the seeds.

In a small saucepan, simmer the wine, shallots, tarragon, rosemary, and salt over medium-high heat until the liquid has been reduced by half. Strain the mixture through a fine sieve.

Scrape the soaked seeds into a food processor. Add the strained wine and process until the mustard turns from liquid and seeds to a creamy mixture flecked with seeds. This takes 3 to 4 minutes. Add additional vinegar as necessary to create a nice creamy mustard. For the best flavor, let this mustard mellow in the refrigerator for about 3 weeks.

Makes about 2¾ cups.

Whole-Grain Mustard
with Whole Dill Seeds

Soaking the dill seeds in vinegar and ale gives this mustard a rich dill flavor. It's wonderful with cheese, in potato salad or deviled eggs, and great with all sorts of meat.

In a nonaluminum pot or jar, combine the mustard seeds, mustard powder, dill seeds, vinegar, and ale; cover and soak for 48 hours, adding additional vinegar and ale (in the correct proportions) if necessary to maintain enough liquid to cover the seeds.

Scrape the soaked seeds into a food processor. Add the salt, sugar, cinnamon, nutmeg, and turmeric and process until the mustard turns from liquid and seeds to a coarse-grained but creamy mixture flecked with seeds. This takes 2 to 3 minutes. Add additional vinegar and ale (in the correct proportions) as necessary to create a nice creamy mustard; keep in mind that it will thicken slightly upon standing. This mustard benefits from two to three weeks of aging.

Makes about 3 cups.

⅔ cup yellow mustard seeds
¼ cup brown mustard seeds
½ cup mustard powder
2 tablespoons dill seeds
¾ cup cider vinegar
¾ cup dark ale
2 teaspoons salt
2 teaspoons sugar
2 teaspoons ground cinnamon
1 teaspoon ground nutmeg
1 teaspoon turmeric

Dilled Pea Salad

One 10-ounce package frozen green
    peas, thawed
⅓ cup chopped scallions, both green
    and white parts
1½ cups shredded and chopped
    green cabbage
½ cup chopped celery
2 hard-boiled eggs, diced
Dilled Dressing (recipe follows)

The first time I had this salad, the chef presented it on individual salad plates. Each serving was generously piled into a hollowed-out tomato, with some of the mixture spilling onto the plate.

Combine the peas, scallions, cabbage, celery, and eggs in a large bowl. Drizzle on enough dressing to thoroughly coat the mixture. Serve chilled.

Makes 8 servings.

Light-supper alternative: You can turn this wonderful little salad into a meal by adding bits of smoked salmon or smoked turkey.

Dilled Dressing

½ cup mayonnaise
½ cup sour cream
1 tablespoon Dilled Mustard (see
    page 52)
2 to 3 teaspoons cider vinegar

Whisk all the ingredients together in a small bowl. This will keep 4 or 5 days in the refrigerator.

Makes about 1 cup.

Salmon Mousse with
Sour Cream~Mustard Sauce

This is an elegant spin-off of the traditional Scandinavian specialty known as fish pudding. Instead of Norwegian codfish, the star in this dish is fresh salmon, with sole and shrimp included for binding purposes (as well as flavoring, of course). Before the advent of the food processor, this dish achieved its light and delicate texture from vigorous beating with a wooden spoon.

Place the salmon, sole, shrimp, and wine in a food processor and process until thoroughly pureed, stopping occasionally to scrape down the sides. Scrape the mixture into a large bowl, cover, and chill for 1 or 2 hours.

Remove the puree from the refrigerator and, using an electric mixer, beat the puree until the consistency has lightened up a bit, 3 or 4 minutes. With the mixer still running, gradually beat in the eggs, cream, cornstarch, salt, pepper, and dill weed and continue beating until the mixture is light and fluffy.

Scrape the fish mixture into a well-buttered 2-quart terrine or loaf pan; gently spread to even it in the pan and remove any air pockets. Place a lightly greased rectangle of waxed paper or parchment on top of the mixture, then seal the pan with a larger piece of aluminum foil, crimping at the outside corners. Place the loaf pan in a larger pan and pour in enough boiling water to come halfway up the sides of the loaf pan. (This technique ensures that your mousse will cook evenly and not dry out.) Bake the mousse in a preheated 400°F oven until the mixture is cooked through, about 1½ hours.

1½ pounds fresh salmon fillets or
  steaks, skinned, deboned, and cut
  into 1-inch chunks
½ pound fillet of sole, cut into
  chunks
¼ pound medium or large shrimp,
  peeled, deveined, and cut into
  chunks
⅓ cup dry white wine
4 large eggs
2 cups heavy cream
4½ teaspoons cornstarch
2¼ teaspoons salt
½ teaspoon ground white pepper
½ teaspoon dillweed
Sour Cream-Mustard Sauce (recipe
  follows)
Sprigs of fresh dill for garnish

Remove the mousse from the oven, then carefully lift it out of the hot water, avoiding the steam—which is very, very hot—and let it rest on a cooling rack for 10 minutes so it can settle a bit. Gently unmold the mousse by placing a serving platter over the top of the mold and then, with a firm hold on the platter and mold, fliping it over. Encourage the mousse to fall from the mold by gently tapping on the pan with a heavy knife handle.

This is delicious served either hot or chilled, with the sour cream-mustard sauce on the side. For an individual serving, spoon a portion of the sauce onto the center of a salad plate, then arrange a slice of the mousse on top, garnishing with a fresh sprig of dill.

Makes about 12 entrée-size servings or 18 half-inch-thick appetizer portions.

1 cup sour cream

¼ cup mayonnaise

3 tablespoons heavy cream

2 tablespoons Swedish Mustard (see page 51)

1 tablespoon fresh lemon juice

½ teaspoon minced fresh dill or a generous pinch of dried, crumbled

Sour Cream Mustard Sauce

Also delicious over steamed vegetables.

Combine all of the ingredients and chill. This will keep in the refrigerator for 4 or 5 days.

Makes about 1½ cups.

European Mustards

18 medium-size fresh shrimp, in
  their shells
1 fresh lobster tail
1 head romaine lettuce
About 1 quart torn iceberg lettuce
  leaves
¼ pound fresh mushrooms, sliced
½ cup shelled fresh peas, blanched
  for 5 minutes in boiling water,
  plunged into cold water to re-
  fresh, and chilled (or simply
  thaw frozen peas)
2 fresh Roma (Italian plum variety) tomatoes, cored and diced
18 fresh asparagus stalks, trimmed,
  blanched for 3 minutes in boiling
  water, drained, and chilled
½ pound fresh (or frozen and
  thawed) crabmeat, picked over
  for cartilage
3 hard-boiled eggs, each cut lengthwise into 6 wedges
6 lemon wedges
Sprigs of fresh dill for garnish
Fresh Herb and Shallot Vinaigrette
  (recipe follows)

Swedish Salad with Herb and Shallot Vinaigrette

This traditional springtime salad from the western coast of Sweden consists of fresh shrimp, crab, lobster, and a plethora of spring greens and vegetables.

Several hours before serving, prepare the shrimp and lobster: Bring a large pot of salted water to a boil. Add the shrimp, still in their shells, and boil just until they have blushed completely pink, then remove them from the pot with a slotted spoon and drain well. Next, add the lobster tail to the boiling water and let boil until it has turned pink. Remove, drain, and chill with the shrimp until ready to assemble the salad.

To assemble the salad, arrange whole romaine leaves on each of 6 dinner plates. Layer on a bed of iceberg. Shell and devein the shrimp, then arrange three on each of the dinner plates. Cut the lobster tail into slices or chunks and divide evenly among the plates. Now divide the remaining ingredients (except the dill and vinaigrette) evenly among the plates, arranging them in an attractive but random manner. Garnish with the dill. Drizzle a bit of the vinaigrette over each serving, then pass the remaining dressing at the table.

Makes 6 servings.

European Mustards

61

Fresh Herb and Shallot Vinaigrette

3 tablespoons white wine vinegar

1 tablespoon Fresh Herb and Shallot Mustard (see page 54)

2 teaspoons capers, drained, rinsed, and chopped

About ½ teaspoon salt

Dash of freshly ground black pepper

½ cup vegetable oil

Whisk together the vinegar, mustard, capers, salt, and pepper, then slowly pour in the oil, whisking all the while. This will keep in the refrigerator at least one week.

Makes about ¾ cup.

Danish Blue Cheese Tart

One 9-inch pastry shell, set into a quiche pan or pie plate

2 tablespoons butter

3 or 4 medium-size yellow onions, thinly sliced

1 cup crumbled Danish blue cheese

2 large eggs

2 large egg yolks

1 cup light cream or half-and-half

¼ teaspoon salt

¼ teaspoon ground white pepper

¼ cup Dilled Mustard (see page 52)

On a warm summer evening, this delectable tart really hits the spot. For an appetizer, shave it into tender little slices, accompanied by crunchy seedless red grapes and a pertinently crisp white Riesling. For a light summer supper, provide a green salad with fresh garden cucumbers and tomatoes tossed in a light vinaigrette.

Place the pastry shell in a preheated 325°F oven and bake for 15 minutes (the pastry will look a bit "sweaty" at this point); remove from the oven.

Melt the butter in a large, heavy skillet over medium heat. Add the onions and cook, stirring, until they are soft and a rich golden brown, 15 to 20 minutes (if you don't rush the process, the onions will caramelize and take on a deep, sweet flavor). Stir in the blue cheese, then remove the pan from the burner and stir until the cheese is melted; set aside. In a small mixing bowl, whisk together the whole eggs, egg yolks, cream, salt, and pepper. Spread the mustard on the bottom of the pie crust, then layer on the onion-cheese mixture. Pour as much of the cream mixture over the onions as possible without overfilling, then bake the tart in a preheated 400°F oven until it is set and lightly golden, about 30 minutes. Remove from the oven, let cool about 10 minutes, then remove the ring if you baked the tart in a quiche pan. Refrigerate until ready to serve. May be prepared up to 24 hours ahead. This tart is delicious served at room temperature or chilled.

Makes one 9-inch tart; 6 entrée servings, 12 first-course servings.

GERMANY

By the twelfth century, mustard had become an important crop in Germany. In fact, since it was comparatively inexpensive, it was labeled "the poor man's spice," as were the other common seasonings of German cuisine, cumin, coriander, fennel, and caraway.

In the mid-eighteenth century, once the special milling process developed in England had reached Germany, German mustards became refined enough to compete with the popular Dijon and Bordeaux styles. The most popular—then and now—is a medium to dark brown condiment laced with golden seeds. It's slightly sweet and quite spicy, yet mild enough to complement a plump Oktoberfest sausage.

As is the case with France's hearty Bordeaux-style mustards, you're more likely to encounter this German specialty alongside a dish than in it. When you're partnering it up with such national treasures as sauerbraten, sauerkraut, or fine Westphalian ham, it's right where it belongs.

German Whole-Grain Mustard

⅔ cup yellow mustard seeds
½ cup brown mustard seeds
¾ cup cider vinegar
¾ cup dark ale
2 cloves garlic, minced
1 teaspoon Worcestershire sauce
2 teaspoons salt
2 teaspoons sugar
2 teaspoons ground allspice
½ teaspoon turmeric

A classic mustard that would be perfectly at home on a slab of crusty bread with juicy chunks of knockwurst on the side. The turmeric provides the blush of gold, so don't leave it out.

In a nonaluminum pot or jar, combine the mustard seeds, vinegar, ale, garlic, and Worcestershire sauce; cover and soak for 48 hours, adding additional vinegar and ale (in the correct proportions) if necessary to maintain enough liquid to cover the seeds.

Scrape the soaked seeds into a food processor. Add the salt, sugar, allspice, and turmeric and process until the mustard turns to a coarse-grained but creamy mixture flecked with seeds. This takes 2 to 3 minutes, so be patient. Add additional vinegar and ale (in the correct proportions) as necessary to create a nice creamy mustard; keep in mind that it will thicken slightly upon standing. This is one mustard I can hardly wait to sample, so letting it age, even for a week or two, is always a challenge. However, giving it a little time to develop in flavor before presenting it to a friend does make it even better.

Makes 2¾ cups.

Sausages with Sauerkraut

Although this is a straightforward, simple combination of hearty and honest ingredients, the sausages and sauerkraut must be treated with respect so their best flavor has an opportunity to shine through.

Rinse the sauerkraut well in a colander, then drain thoroughly. Place the bacon in the bottom of a deep-sided 2-quart glass casserole dish. Place the sauerkraut on top of the bacon, then sprinkle the onion over the top. Pour in enough chicken broth to just cover the sauerkraut, cover, and bake in a preheated 350°F oven for 1 hour.

Meanwhile, place the kielbasa and the scallions in a skillet with enough beer to cover it. Bring the mixture to a boil, then reduce the heat to medium-low and simmer about 45 minutes.

While the kielbasa is cooking, place the bratwursts and knockwursts in another skillet with enough beer to cover them, bring to a boil, then reduce the heat to medium and simmer for 10 minutes. Remove the sausages from the beer. Pour off the beer, then add the butter to the skillet and melt over medium heat. Add the bratwursts and cook until golden brown on all sides.

To serve, remove the cooked sauerkraut from the casserole with a slotted spoon and arrange on a large platter, surrounded by the cooked sausages. Spoon on some of the cooking liquid from the sauerkraut. The larger sausages should be cut into thick slices and the smaller sausages halved. Serve with a choice of hearty mustards. Baked potatoes or crusty French bread, as well as a crunchy tossed green salad, would round out the meal. Be sure to have plenty of chilled beer or ale on hand.

Makes 8 servings.

2 pounds fresh-packed sauerkraut (available in the refrigerator section of fine-quality supermarkets and delicatessens), rinsed and drained

6 strips thickly sliced bacon

1½ cups coarsely diced onion

2½ cups canned or homemade chicken broth

1 large kielbasa sausage

2 cups chopped scallions, both green and white parts

About 3 cups dark beer

8 bratwursts

4 knockwursts

2 tablespoons butter or margarine

German Whole-Grain Mustard (see page 64) and other mustards of your choice

GREAT BRITAIN

The English lean toward a fiery mustard, much like a full-bodied Dijon—smooth and creamy, with a steamy kick to the sinuses.

Throughout medieval times, most mustard was made either in the home or in monasteries. But by the early 1500s, Tewkesbury, in Gloucestershire, became widely known as the mustard-making capital of England. Tewkesbury mustard was hotter than most due to the fresh horseradish the manufacturers were fond of stirring into it. But what really set this mustard apart was its unique shape. After the seeds were ground and sifted, flour was combined with the seasonings and horseradish, and the stiff paste was formed into balls. Once purchased, it could keep in a kitchen for an indefinite period of time. As needed, the mistress of the house would break off a chunk from the ball and reconstitute it by stirring in a liquid, be it vinegar, wine, or fruit juice. The fact that it was formed and sold in balls made it easy to transport. Needless to say, it was a mighty mustard.

Once Jeremiah Colman was appointed "Manufacturer of Mustard to Her Majesty" by Queen Victoria in 1866, his business exploded. By 1869, one day's production required a train with four boxcars to transport it from the factory. To this day, Colman's mustard-yellow can with the red bull is a familiar image worldwide.

As in other parts of the world, however, Colman has had to make room for a newer breed of mustard makers. These days, a fine-tuned British mustard continues to pack a wallop. In fact, some of the smaller manufacturers are reinstating the use of horseradish as an ingredient, while others are flavoring their batches with English wine and ale. What hasn't changed is mustard's popularity at the neighborhood public meeting house. Any pub worth its salt will offer its clientele a broad selection of mustards, or at least three or four. If they aren't within arm's reach on the tables, you can be sure that a collection of mustard pots is a permanent fixture on the bar.

Spicy English Pub Mustard

Admittedly, this is not as potent as the Tewkesbury mustard balls of times past. Nevertheless, with nothing but a little ale to soften its punch, this one can still knock the uninitiated palate clear back to the American Revolution.

1 cup English mustard powder
  (Colman's is a reliable brand)
¾ cup light or dark ale
½ teaspoon salt

Combine the mustard, ale, and salt and refrigerate at least 24 hours before using.

Makes 2 scant cups.

Grandma Skinner's Luncheon Scones

On most Sunday afternoons in my early years, we could generally expect my Great-Aunt Meg and Uncle Ron to come visit my Grandma Skinner. Being of Scottish descent, my grandmother would invariably whip up a batch of griddle scones for her sister and brother-in-law and serve them with lunch. As you may know, scones are Britain's contribution to the biscuit genre—and one of the best devices known for transporting strawberry jam from jar to mouth. But during these meals, the toasty little morsels were the vehicle for whatever sandwich filling we happened to have on hand. This could be a Welsh rarebit Grandma would prepare with milk, cheese, and eggs, or, more often, a ham of some sort with a well-aged cheddar. The jar of English mustard was never far from reach.

3 cups all-purpose flour
1½ teaspoons salt
1½ teaspoons baking soda
1½ teaspoons cream of tartar
1 teaspoon sugar
1 tablespoon butter
1½ cups buttermilk
Sandwich fillings: sliced ham, sliced
   cheese, tomatoes
Spicy English Pub Mustard (see
   page 67)

Sift all of the dry ingredients together into a bowl. By hand, rub the butter into the flour until it forms small, cornmeal-like granules. Add the buttermilk all at once. Working quickly but gently, mix with a dinner knife (a spoon will overwork the dough, making a tough scone) until the dough is just barely mixed. Add a little more buttermilk if necessary, but don't let the dough become sticky.

Divide the dough into quarters. On a floured board, roll out each quarter into a circle ¼ inch thick. Cut each circle into quarters. Heat a griddle to 350°F; test it by flicking drops of water on the surface. The water will dance across the griddle and evaporate within about 3 to 4 seconds when it's hot enough. Bake the scones in batches on the lightly greased griddle for a few minutes, until each is lightly golden on the bottom. Turn and cook the other side. Now, if desired, brown all of the edges in turn by standing the triangles up and leaning them against each other for about 30 seconds. As the scones come off the griddle, cool in a tea towel until ready to use.

As I said, Scottish scones are delicious straight off the griddle with butter and fresh strawberry jam or lemon curd. But if you can hold off long enough for them to cool, slice them open with a serrated knife; fill with ham, sliced cheese, and sliced tomatoes; and slather with mustard.

Makes 16 scones.

Cumberland Sauce

1 cup red currant jelly
Grated rind of 2 lemons
Grated rind of 2 oranges
2 tablespoons confectioner's sugar
2 tablespoons port wine
1 tablespoon *Spicy English Pub Mustard (see page 67)*

An English tradition, Cumberland sauce is fabulous with game, but I also consider it a proper accompaniment to baked ham, as well as roast lamb and chicken. Certainly, a sauce that's been around as long as this one will have numerous variations. The following is one that I obtained from my cousin Ron Crawford, an avid hunter who also happens to be a terrific cook. This recipe was first published in his own cookbook, *Ron Crawford's Cookbook.*

Melt the jelly in a saucepan over medium heat with the lemon and orange rinds. Whisk in the sugar, port, and mustard. Simmer gently over medium heat for about 1 minute, then remove from the heat.

Makes about 1¾ cups.

RUSSIA

Some of the finest mustard seeds are produced in Russia, which also is among the world's largest growers. As in Germany, the cuisine of Russia lends itself beautifully to this piquant condiment, since it is such a marvelous counterpoint to the rich sausages and savory pastries of the region. The meat-filled dumpling known as *vereniki*—a Russian version of the Chinese dim sum—once lifted from its vat of cooking water, is particularly delicious when a generous dollop of a hot and sweet Russian mustard is within dipping distance. Similarly, the elegant but hearty piroshki, another savory hand-held pie of Russian origin, should always be served with a bit of mustard.

Sweet and Hot Russian Mustard

Prepare the Classic Dijon mustard, substituting the vodka for the white wine and omitting the mace and cinnamon. After the mustard has been pressed through a sieve, stir in the brown sugar. This mustard will need about 2 weeks to develop its flavor.

Makes 2 scant cups.

1 recipe Classic Dijon (see page 20, and read instructions here before preparing it)
½ cup vodka
½ cup firmly packed light brown sugar

Piroshki

These mushroom-laden morsels take a little more effort to prepare than meat loaf, but if you can find the time, you won't be sorry.

Place the flour in a food processor. Add the chilled butter pieces and cut into the flour by pulsing until the butter is coarsely chopped. Add the cream cheese and continue to pulse in short, quick spurts until the mixture forms a ball that will hold its shape when pressed together. If you prepare this by hand, cut the butter into the flour with a pastry blender or two knives, then blend in the cream cheese, mixing until the dough forms a ball that holds its shape.

With lightly floured hands, on a lightly floured work surface, pat the dough into a round; wrap in plastic and refrigerate about 1 hour.

While the dough is chilling, prepare the filling. Bring the potatoes to a boil with water to cover and boil until tender, 20 to 25 minutes. Remove from the heat and drain. When cool enough to handle, peel and dice into ¼-inch cubes to measure 1 cup. Melt the remaining 2 tablespoons of butter and the oil in a large skillet. Add the onion and shallots and cook briefly over medium-high heat, stirring. Add the

1 cup all-purpose flour
½ cup (1 stick) well-chilled butter, cut into 12 pieces
4 ounces cream cheese
2 or 3 medium-size white or red boiling potatoes
2 tablespoons butter
1 tablespoon vegetable oil
2 tablespoons finely minced onion
2 shallots, finely minced
¾ pound mushrooms, finely minced (a food processor works well)
⅓ cup Madeira wine
½ teaspoon dried thyme, crumbled
¼ teaspoon salt
¼ teaspoon ground white pepper
About 3 tablespoons heavy cream
Sweet and Hot Russian Mustard (see above)
German Whole-Grain Mustard (see page 64)

mushrooms and continue to cook, stirring frequently, until all of the liquid that is released from the mushrooms has evaporated, 15 to 20 minutes. Once the mushrooms are darkened and dry, add the Madeira, thyme, salt, and pepper. Continue to cook until the liquid has evaporated and the mixture is thick again, about 15 more minutes. Stir in the potatoes, then adjust the seasonings. Let the mixture cool thoroughly before using.

Roll the dough on a floured work surface to about ⅛- to ¼-inch thickness. Cut into 6-inch circles. Continue rerolling and cutting the scraps to create as many circles as you can. You should end up with about 18 circles.

To fill, place a spoonful of the cooled filling off-center on each circle, then fold the circle in half over the filling, pressing the edges together firmly to seal. To create a firm seal, crimp all around the edges with the tines of a fork.

Arrange the piroshki on ungreased baking sheets and brush the tops with the heavy cream. Bake in a preheated 400°F oven until golden, about 25 minutes. Serve hot or at room temperature, with a zesty collection of hearty mustards.

Makes about 18 piroshki.

Note: The piroshki may be prepared, baked, then refrigerated up to 48 hours ahead of time; reheat in a preheated 400°F oven for about 10 minutes. Frozen piroshki should be thawed before reheating. To reheat, simply bake in a 400°F oven until heated through, about 10 to 15 minutes.

Kraut Kunchen

1 cup milk, heated to lukewarm
½ cup warm water (95° to 100°F)
1½ teaspoons dry yeast
2 teaspoons sugar
4 to 5 cups all-purpose flour
1 teaspoon salt
6 tablespoons (¾ stick) butter, at
   room temperature
1¼ pounds ground beef
½ cup chopped onion
4 cups chopped green cabbage
Freshly ground black pepper to taste
Maggi seasoning to taste
About 2 teaspoons chicken base
   (available in the supermarket
   spice section)
Sweet and Hot Russian Mustard
   (see page 71), for dipping

Leif Eric Benson, executive chef at Timberline Lodge, Oregon's historic resort at the base of Mount Hood, has been delighting diners for years with this favorite. Prepare it full-size for an entrée, or mini-size for delicious appetizers. In either case, Sweet and Hot Russian Mustard is the perfect condiment.

Combine the milk and hot water, then sprinkle on the yeast and sugar. Let the mixture sit until it bubbles and foams, 5 to 10 minutes.

Stir in 3 cups of the flour, the salt, and the butter, then turn out onto a floured board and knead in enough of the remaining flour to achieve a smooth and elastic dough. This should take about 10 minutes. Place the dough in a lightly oiled bowl, turn once to coat, cover loosely with plastic wrap, and allow to rise in a warm place until doubled in volume, about 90 minutes.

Meanwhile, brown the beef in a large skillet over medium-high heat. Partway through the cooking, remove the drippings, add the onion, and continue to cook until the onion is tender. Add the cabbage and remaining seasonings, stirring to mix well; adjust the seasonings, adding more salt if necessary.

For entrée-size portions, divide the dough into 6 parts. On a floured board with a floured rolling pin, roll out each part into a 10-inch round. Place a heaping ½ cup of filling on one half of each round. For appetizer-size portions, divide the dough into 12 parts and roll each part into a 5-inch round. Place a heaping ¼ cup of filling on half of each. Fold over and seal. Bake in a preheated 350°F oven until golden brown, about 30 minutes for the entrée size, 20 minutes for the appetizer size. Serve hot or chilled with the Russian mustard.

Makes 6 entrée servings, 12 appetizer servings.

Chapter Four

The Pacific Rim
and Beyond to India—
A Balance of Fire and Flavor

Come on an exotic voyage into the world of the Pacific Rim—and beyond—where a condiment such as mustard is so often an integral part of the dining experience. In China, flavors, colors, and textures are a study in contrast and harmony, yin and yang. A saucer of fiery-hot mustard paste becomes an essential counterpoint to the blander preparations of noodles, rice, and dumplings. For the Japanese, fiery-hot becomes molten when the shredded root of the wasabe plant is stirred into a mustard dipping sauce.

As each cuisine in this region has evolved—particularly within the context of "East meets West"—mustards have taken on an important role, serving as potent partners to such Pacific Rim specialties as pineapple, macadamia nuts, cilantro, ginger root, sesame oil, coconut, dried mushrooms, and chili oil.

Chinese Toasted Sesame Mustard

½ cup yellow mustard seeds

½ cup brown mustard seeds

½ cup mustard powder

2 cups rice vinegar

⅔ cup water

4 cloves garlic, minced

½ cup sesame seeds, toasted (see note below)

1 tablespoon sesame oil (see note below)

2½ teaspoons salt

In a nonaluminum pot or jar, combine the mustard seeds, mustard powder, vinegar, water, and garlic. Cover and soak for 48 hours, adding additional vinegar and water (in the correct proportions) if necessary to maintain enough liquid to cover the seeds.

Scrape the soaked seeds mixture into a food processor. Add the sesame seeds, sesame oil, and salt and process until the mustard turns from liquid and seeds to a creamy mixture flecked with seeds. This takes about 3 to 4 minutes. Add additional vinegar and water (in the correct proportions) as necessary to create a nice creamy mustard; keep in mind that it will thicken slightly upon standing. This mustard benefits from at least one week of aging.

Makes about 3½ cups.

Note: To toast the sesame seeds, place them in a dry skillet and cook over medium to medium-high heat, shaking the pan frequently, until they begin to turn golden and start "popping."

Look for sesame oil with the other cooking oils in your supermarket, or in the oriental-food section.

Japanese Wasabe Mustard

HOT! HOT! HOT!

In a small bowl, whisk together the mustard powder, water, and soy sauce. Let the mixture sit for a few moments to determine whether additional water is needed to reach the desired consistency. Whisk in the sesame oil and wasabe powder. This mustard is at the height of its potency immediately after being prepared.

Makes 1 scant cup.

½ cup mustard powder (see note below)

About ⅓ cup cold water

2 teaspoons soy sauce

2 teaspoons sesame oil (see note on page 78)

1 teaspoon Japanese wasabe powder (see note below)

Note: A Japanese mustard powder will yield the hottest paste, since it's made entirely from black mustard seeds, but a Chinese mustard powder (which is usually a blend of yellow and brown seeds) will do just fine. If you want to use Japanese mustard and can't find it at your local spice shop, check Sources at the back of this book.

Wasabe is a powder derived from a Japanese-style horseradish; it is available in the specialty-food section of well-stocked supermarkets or stores specializing in oriental foods.

Chili-Garlic Mustard

Chili-garlic sauce is a Chinese condiment that can be found in the specialty-food section of most supermarkets. It has a deep red-orange color and a zesty flavor. A good brand to use is Sun Luck.

½ cup yellow mustard seeds
½ cup brown mustard seeds
¾ cup cider vinegar
¼ cup water
3 tablespoons chili-garlic sauce
1 teaspoon salt

In a nonaluminum pot or jar, combine the mustard seeds, vinegar, and water; cover and soak for 48 hours, adding additional vinegar and water (in the correct proportions) if necessary to maintain enough liquid to cover the seeds.

Scrape the soaked seeds into a food processor. Add the chili-garlic sauce and salt and process until the mustard turns from liquid and seeds to a creamy mixture flecked with seeds. This takes 3 to 4 minutes. Add additional vinegar and water (in the correct proportions) as necessary to create a nice creamy mustard; keep in mind that it will thicken slightly upon standing. I can rarely wait long enough to give this wonderful mustard any aging time, and that seems to be perfectly all right.

Makes about 2⅓ cups.

Toasted Macadamia Nut Mustard

½ cup yellow mustard seeds

3 tablespoons brown mustard seeds

1 cup rice vinegar

¼ cup water

3 cloves garlic, chopped

1 cup macadamia nuts, coarsely chopped and toasted (see note on page 43)

¼ cup firmly packed light brown sugar

2 teaspoons salt

1 teaspoon ground cinnamon

1 teaspoon peeled and shredded fresh ginger

¼ teaspoon ground mace

In a nonaluminum pot or jar, combine the mustard seeds, vinegar, water, and garlic; cover and soak for 48 hours, adding additional vinegar and water (in the correct proportions) if necessary to maintain enough liquid to cover the seeds.

Scrape the soaked seeds into a food processor. Add the remaining ingredients, then process until the mustard turns from liquid and seeds to a creamy mixture flecked with seeds. The macadamia nut bits will eventually puree into a homogeneous mixture, blending splendidly with the mustard. The process takes at least 3 to 4 minutes. Add additional vinegar and water (in the correct proportions) if necessary to create a nice creamy mustard; keep in mind that it will thicken slightly upon standing. This mustard can be consumed immediately.

Makes about 2 cups.

Coconut Cream Variation: Stir in 3 tablespoons of coconut cream (available in the liquor-supply section of the supermarket). The rich and toasty flavor of the macadamia nuts is enhanced by the nutty taste of the coconut.

Hot and Zesty Oriental Mustard

Straight from the jar, this makes a quick and simple dipping sauce for spring rolls, pot stickers, and any number of oriental nibbles.

In a small bowl, whisk together the mustard powder and vinegar until the mustard is smooth and creamy. Whisk in the remaining ingredients. Refrigerate for at least 1 hour before using.

Makes 2 cups.

1½ cups mustard powder
¾ cup rice vinegar
¼ cup soy sauce
¼ cup chili sauce (look for it in the supermarket near the ketchup)
2 tablespoons sesame oil (see note on page 78)
1 tablespoon white wine Worcestershire sauce (this gives the mustard a nice sheen)

Creamy Curry Mustard

In Indian cuisine, you're more likely to find whole mustard seeds, swimming around in a zesty dish of curry, than you are to encounter prepared mustard. However, curry—the seasoning—stands up so beautifully to homemade mustard that I couldn't pass up the opportunity to stir it into some. The combination's delicious in a chicken salad with apples, raisins, scallions, cherry tomatoes, and just a dollop of mayonnaise.

In a small bowl, whisk together the mustard powder, vinegar, water, and salt until the mustard is smooth and creamy. In a small skillet, heat the sesame oil over medium heat, then add the onion and garlic and cook, stirring, until the onion is soft and translucent. Sprinkle in the curry powder and continue cooking for about 1 minute; remove from the heat and cool slightly (the onion should still be warm, but not sizzling-hot). Scrape the mustard and onion mixtures into a food processor and puree until smooth and creamy. Refrigerate for at least 1 hour before using.

Makes 2 cups.

1½ cups mustard powder
¾ cup rice vinegar
¼ cup water
2 teaspoons salt
2 tablespoons sesame oil (see note on page 78)
½ cup finely minced onion
3 cloves garlic, finely minced
1 tablespoon good-quality curry powder

Coconut Cream with Rum Mustard

One 2-ounce tin (about ½ cup)
Colman's Whole Grain Mustard
(see note below)

¼ cup dark rum

¼ cup distilled vinegar

¼ teaspoon salt

2 tablespoons coconut cream (available in the liquor-supply section of the supermarket)

This may sound like an unusual (okay, odd!) combination, but the flavors really work well together and are particularly delicious alongside a baked ham or grilled pork chops. Whisk a spoonful into some heavy cream, and you've got a simple sauce for grilled fish.

In a small bowl, combine the mustard, rum, and vinegar. Stir until the mixture is well combined (it will appear quite soupy at this point), cover, and let soak for 24 hours so the seeds and powder can absorb the liquid. Stir in the salt and coconut cream. This is ready to use immediately.

Makes about ⅔ cup.

Note: Colman's Whole Grain Mustard is a dry mustard blend that contains both powder and whole mustard seeds.

Spinach Salad with Toasted Macadamia Nut Mustard Vinaigrette and Maui Onions

Fresh spinach lends itself to so many different salad combinations that it's pretty hard to go wrong.

In a beautiful large salad bowl, combine the spinach, macadamia nuts, onion, avocados, and pineapple. Gently toss the salad with enough of the dressing to generously coat all of the ingredients. Serve immediately.

Makes 8 servings.

8 cups *fresh spinach leaves, thoroughly washed and dried, and torn into bite-size pieces (with the tough stems removed)*

1½ cups *macadamia nuts, lightly toasted (see note on page 43) and coarsely chopped*

1 *Maui or other sweet Spanish-style onion, sliced into rings*

2 *avocados (preferably the pebbly-skinned Haas variety), peeled, pitted, and sliced or diced*

½ cup *fresh pineapple, cut into ½-inch cubes*

Toasted Macadamia Nut Mustard Vinaigrette (recipe follows)

Toasted Macadamia Nut Mustard Vinaigrette

In a small bowl, combine the vinegar, mustard, and brown sugar and season with salt and pepper. Whisk in the oils. Adjust the seasonings (depending on your taste, it may need a bit more brown sugar to achieve the desired sweet-and-sour balance). This dressing will keep up to 2 weeks in the refrigerator.

Makes about ¾ cup.

¼ cup *rice vinegar*

2 tablespoons *Toasted Macadamia Nut Mustard (see page 82)*

1 teaspoon *firmly packed light brown sugar*

Sprinkling of salt and freshly ground black pepper

⅓ cup *vegetable oil*

2 tablespoons *sesame oil (see note on page 78)*

Embutido

2 pounds ground pork
1½ pounds chorizo sausage, casings removed and meat crumbled
3 tablespoons diced canned pimiento
1 cup shredded carrot
1 cup chopped onion
5 large cloves garlic, finely minced
4 large eggs
1 cup sweet pickle relish
1½ cups plain bread crumbs
3 tablespoons soy sauce
1 teaspoon salt
½ teaspoon freshly ground black pepper
Chinese Toasted Sesame Mustard (see page 78) and Chili-Garlic Mustard (see page 81) for dipping
Ketchup for dipping

For several years, Nettie, a Filipino friend, would make these flavorful loaves of sausage for us every time she knew we were throwing a special event. Since she always baked more than enough, I discovered early on that they freeze beautifully. It's a classic dish in the Philippines, apparently adapted from a Spanish preparation called *galantina*.

Combine all the ingredients except the dips in a large bowl. Divide the mixture into 4 equal portions. Shape each portion into a 10-inch log, pressing the meat mixture firmly into place to remove any air pockets. Roll each log in a sheet of heavy-duty aluminum foil, twisting the foil closed at both ends.

Place the rolls in a foil-lined baking pan (if you line the pan with foil you'll avoid a horrendous cleanup) and bake in a preheated 400°F oven for 1 hour. Remove the pan from the oven and let the rolls cool undisturbed in the baking pan for about 45 minutes, then place them in the refrigerator for at least 24 hours before serving. (Note: If the cooked rolls aren't allowed to firm up for a day, they will crumble when sliced.)

To serve, unroll each log and slice into desired-size pieces or chunks. Arrange on a large platter with thinly sliced baguette rounds and a small bowl of each of the mustards and the ketchup.

Makes enough to serve about 20 people as an appetizer.

Chinese Spring Rolls

There's no denying the fact that spring rolls represent a serious commitment of time and labor, but they're worth it! Several years ago I encouraged my younger son—the one with the picky palate—to help in the preparation phase. He became so enchanted with the colorful melange of fresh produce and flavorful meat that he actually ate the finished product.

Heat the 2 tablespoons of oil in a large frying pan or wok over medium-high to high heat. Add the onion, leek, celery, jalapeño, garlic, and ginger and stir-fry for about 1 minute. Add the pork, cabbage, and bamboo shoots and continue to stir-fry for an additional 3 or 4 minutes. In a small bowl, blend together the sherry, soy sauce, and cornstarch. Stir the mixture into the vegetables and cook just until thickened. Do not overcook or the vegetables will not be crunchy. Remove from the heat, adjust the seasonings, and cool thoroughly before proceeding. The filling can be made up to 48 hours ahead.

For each spring roll, place an egg roll skin on a flat surface, with a corner pointing toward you. Arrange about 2 rounded tablespoons of the filling horizontally across the skin to within 1 inch of the left and right corners. Fold the corner nearest you over the filling. Brush a dot of beaten egg on the left and right corners, then fold these corners in over the filling, pressing them firmly down onto the previously folded corner. Now roll the package to within 1 inch of the top corner. Dot the top corner with beaten egg and press it down on the roll to seal. As each spring roll is completed, cover it with plastic wrap until ready to fry. The rolls can be refrigerated up to 12 hours before frying (or frozen for several months; they don't need to be thawed before frying).

Heat about 2 inches of oil in a wok, deep fryer, or high-sided skillet

2 tablespoons vegetable oil

1 cup chopped onion

½ cup chopped leek, the white part plus some of the pale green, if you wish

1 cup thinly sliced celery

1 jalapeño pepper, seeded and minced

2 cloves garlic, minced or pressed

½ teaspoon peeled and minced fresh ginger

1 pound Chinese barbecued pork (available in well-stocked delis; or substitute quality smoked ham), cut into very thin strips

2 cups finely shredded cabbage

One 5-ounce can bamboo shoots, cut into very thin strips

3 tablespoons dry sherry

1 tablespoon soy sauce

1 tablespoon cornstarch

One 1-pound package egg roll skins (available in the oriental-food section of a well-stocked produce department)

1 large egg, beaten

Additional vegetable oil, preferably peanut oil

Chinese Toasted Sesame Mustard (see page 78) and Hot and Zesty Oriental Mustard (page 83) for dipping

to 350°F over medium-high heat. To test the temperature, touch the bottom of the pan with a chopstick. If tiny bubbles dance up from beneath the tip, it's hot enough; if it bubbles furiously, it's too hot. Slip a few of the spring rolls at a time into the hot oil and fry until golden, turning to brown evenly on all sides. After frying, drain well on paper towels and serve immediately, or refrigerate for later use. Spring rolls are equally delicious hot or cold.

Cooked spring rolls can also be wrapped and frozen. To reheat frozen rolls, place them on an ungreased baking sheet and bake in a preheated 375°F oven for about 20 minutes, or microwave on high until heated through (microwaving, however, won't result in a crisp coating).

Serve the spring rolls with small bowls of the mustards on hand for dipping.

Makes about 30 spring rolls.

Grilled Albacore in Mustard-Sesame Marinade

½ cup olive oil

¼ cup finely minced cilantro (fresh coriander)

¼ cup Chinese Toasted Sesame Mustard (see page 78)

½ teaspoon salt

¼ teaspoon freshly ground black pepper

4 albacore or yellowfin tuna steaks, each weighing 6 or 7 ounces

Albacore is a firm-fleshed and relatively mild fish that works with a variety of sauces and marinades. Another excellent type to use is yellowfin tuna. In this recipe, the sesame-ginger combination in the mustard is particularly wonderful.

In a small bowl, whisk together the oil, cilantro, mustard, salt, and black pepper. Pour the mixture over the tuna steaks and let marinate in the refrigerator for 1 hour.

Grill the steaks over medium-hot coals, cooking for about 3 minutes on each side, depending on the thickness. When done, the fish will have just barely become opaque all the way through, with the pinkness just beginning to disappear at the center. It will continue to cook after being removed from the heat, so removing it at this stage will prevent the tuna from overcooking.

Makes 4 servings.

Hawaiian Crab Cakes with Toasted Macadamia Nut Mustard Sauce

¼ cup olive oil

1½ cups finely minced celery

1 cup finely minced onion

¼ cup seeded and finely minced red bell pepper

1 teaspoon peeled and grated fresh ginger

6 slices white bread, trimmed and torn into ¼-inch pieces

1 cup milk

An elegant hors d'oeuvre or light supper. East Coast cooks don't have a monopoly on the crab cake concept. Wherever you find a supply of fresh crabs, you're going to have cooks combining them with other regional ingredients. Because this version is baked rather than fried, the fat content is considerably lower than in some recipes you may have encountered.

Heat the oil in a skillet over medium heat. Add the celery, onion, bell pepper, and ginger and cook, stirring, until the onion is translucent. Remove from the heat and set aside.

Meanwhile, combine the bread with the milk and let sit for about 5 minutes. Drain the bread, squeezing it well (reserve the milk). In a mixing bowl, combine the bread, sautéed vegetables, crabmeat, eggs, cilantro, mustard, salt, and pepper. Add some of the reserved milk, if necessary, to create a mixture that is relatively firm but moist.

Form the crab mixture into 2-inch-diameter balls, pressing gently with your hands to flatten the balls slightly into thick cakes. Roll each cake in the bread crumbs until evenly coated and then arrange on a lightly greased baking sheet, leaving at least 1 inch between each cake. Bake in a preheated 400°F oven until golden brown, about 15 minutes.

To serve, either arrange all of the crab cakes on a large platter with the sauce, or place on individual plates with dollops of sauce on the side. Garnish with cilantro leaves.

**Makes 1 dozen 3-inch crab cakes
(enough to serve 6 people as an entrée).**

*1½ pounds fresh or frozen and
  thawed crabmeat, well drained
4 large eggs, lightly beaten
1 tablespoon finely minced cilantro
  (fresh coriander)
2 teaspoons Toasted Macadamia
  Nut Mustard (see page 82)
½ teaspoon salt
¼ teaspoon ground white pepper
2 cups plain bread crumbs
Additional cilantro leaves for
  garnish
Toasted Macadamia Nut Mustard
  Sauce (recipe follows)*

Toasted Macadamia Nut Mustard Sauce

In a small bowl, whisk together all the ingredients. This sauce will keep at least one week in the refrigerator. Try using it as a tangy sandwich spread or vegetable dip.

Makes 1¼ scant cups.

*¾ cup mayonnaise
¼ cup buttermilk
¼ cup finely minced scallions, both
  green and white parts
1 tablespoon Toasted Macadamia
  Nut Mustard (see page 82)*

Pork Tenderloin in Mustard-Soy Marinade

1½ to 2 pounds pork tenderloin (about 2 to 3 average-size strips, depending on their size)

½ cup tempura sauce (see note on page 94)

½ cup water

2 tablespoons Toasted Macadamia Nut Mustard (see page 82), Hot and Zesty Oriental Mustard (page 83), or Japanese Wasabe Mustard (page 79)

½ cup (1 stick) butter

Those exquisitely tender strips of pork tenderloin, although dear in price, make a wonderful presentation. You'll rarely find them on special, and some stores don't even carry them. But here's a simple yet stunning preparation if you ever care to indulge yourself and your guests.

Place the tenderloins in a shallow, narrow container or resealable plastic bag. In a separate bowl, combine the tempura sauce, water, and mustard. Pour the marinade over the tenderloins and let marinate in the refrigerator at least 3 hours but not more than 12.

About 15 minutes before serving, remove the tenderloins from the marinade. In a small pan, melt the butter with ⅓ cup of the marinade over low heat. Remove from the heat. Brush the tenderloins with some of the tempura butter, then place them on the grill over hot coals. Although the long, narrow tenderloins are somewhat round, treat them as if they have four sides. After 5 minutes, brush with the tempura butter again, then turn so the top sides are now on the bottom, and baste again. After 5 more minutes, baste, then turn each of the tenderloins onto one of the uncooked sides; baste again. After about 3 minutes, baste, then turn each onto the remaining uncooked side; baste and cook about 3 more minutes. Total cooking time will be about 16 minutes at this point, which should be sufficient. The interior will retain a bit of pink at this stage but should be almost gray. If not, cook about 2 more minutes. Remove from the grill, and let the meat stand for 5 minutes (it will continue cooking until it cools somewhat, so don't overcook it on the coals). To serve, cut the tenderloins into 1- or 2-inch-thick slices.

If you want some extra dipping sauce, gently simmer the remaining marinade (not the basting sauce) over medium heat for 10 minutes and serve at the table.

Makes 4 to 6 servings.

Sugar Snap Pea Salad with Toasted Sesame Seed Dressing

The sugar snap pea lends itself beautifully to the light touch of oriental cuisine. It isn't like the common shell pea, nor is it like the edible-pod snow pea typically used in oriental stir-fry dishes. This relatively new variety is a combination of both. With its normal-size peas, it looks a lot like the shell pea. But the pod wall is specially bred to be low in fiber and very, very sweet. The result is a plump little vegetable that can be popped into your mouth raw, pod and all.

It's pretty hard to wreck a sugar snap pea, as long as you don't overcook it; they're best raw or just barely blanched. I prefer to either quickly stir-fry them in a bit of oil, or place them in a colander and pour boiling water over them. (If chilling is required, then a plunge into cold water after the colander treatment would be in order.)

Pare the stem end from each sugar snap pea. Place the peas in a large colander, then pour about 2 quarts boiling water over them to just barely blanch the peas. Have a large pot of cold water waiting so you can immediately plunge the peas into it to stop the cooking and set the color. Drain well and chill until ready to assemble the salad.

1 pound fresh sugar snap peas

2 to 3 tablespoons sesame oil (see note on page 78)

2 to 3 tablespoons light-flavored vegetable oil

2 teaspoons mustard (any of the mustards from this chapter would add their own unique flavor)

2 teaspoons soy sauce

½ teaspoon peeled and finely minced fresh ginger

¼ cup sesame seeds, toasted (see note on page 78)

About 1 tablespoon finely minced cilantro (fresh coriander)

Just before serving, whisk together the two oils with the mustard, soy sauce, and ginger. Toss this mixture with the peas and pile them into a beautiful bowl or platter. Garnish with the sesame seeds and cilantro and serve.

Makes 4 to 6 servings.

⅓ cup fresh lime juice

3 tablespoons tempura sauce (see note below)

1 teaspoon peeled and grated fresh ginger

1 teaspoon Chinese Toasted Sesame Mustard (see page 78)

1 clove garllic, minced

⅔ cup vegetable oil

¾ pound dried somen, soba, or other thin oriental noodles

½ pound cooked tiny fresh Pacific shrimp (if unavailable, substitute fresh or fresh-frozen medium shrimp that you have peeled, deveined, steamed or boiled until pink and opaque, and diced into ½-inch cubes)

6 scallions, chopped

2 tablespoons sesame seeds, toasted (see note on page 78)

Somen Noodle Salad with Pacific Shrimp

Japanese somen noodles, made from rice flour, are very thin and are often sold in bundles, bound with brocade tape. If they aren't available in the oriental-food section of your supermarket, look for them in an oriental specialty-food store. If the package doesn't offer cooking instructions, begin testing for doneness just a minute or two after the noodles have been placed in a large pot of boiling salted water.

Combine the lime juice, tempura sauce, ginger, mustard, garlic, and oil in a large serving bowl. Refrigerate until ready to use.

Cook the noodles in 4 quarts of boiling water until just barely tender. Drain well, rinse, and drain again. Toss the noodles with the prepared lime dressing. Gently fold in the shrimp, scallions, and sesame seeds. Refrigerate about 1 hour before serving. Can be prepared up to 6 hours ahead.

Makes 12 salad servings.

Note: Look for tempura sauce next to the soy sauce in the supermarket. A good brand is Kikkoman.

When asparagus come into season in your area, you could steam about ¼ pound until crisp-tender, then cut them into bite-size pieces and toss in with the salad.

Gingered Beef

You must be a fan of fresh ginger to enjoy this spicy entrée. Stick the leftover knob of ginger root in the freezer when you're through with it. Sealed in plastic wrap, it keeps for months. For future recipes, it's easy to grate the desired amount from the rock-hard frozen root.

Partially freeze the flank steak (freeze for about 20 minutes) to facilitate thin slicing. Cut the steak diagonally, across the grain, into very thin strips.

Whisk together the cornstarch, soy sauce, sesame oil, mustard, and pepper flakes. Marinate the beef slices in this mixture for 30 minutes in the refrigerator.

Meanwhile, in a small bowl, toss together the ginger and salt; let stand for 20 minutes. Squeeze the ginger shreds to extract most of their moisture, then set aside.

Combine the sugar and sherry; set aside.

When the beef has marinated, heat the peanut oil in a wok or skillet over medium heat. Add the drained meat, stirring to separate the pieces. When the pieces change color, remove them to a colander to drain. (Some of the meat might still be pink.)

Remove all but about 3 tablespoons of the oil from the pan. (The oil can be strained and saved for another use, if refrigerated.) Heat the oil, then add the reserved ginger. Stir rapidly for 15 seconds. Add the beef; cook, stirring, for 15 seconds. Stir in the cilantro leaves and sugar-sherry mixture. Cook just until the dish is heated through.

Makes 4 servings.

1 pound beef flank steak
1 tablespoon cornstarch
1 tablespoon soy sauce
1 tablespoon sesame oil (see note on page 78)
1 tablespoon Japanese Wasabe Mustard (see page 79) or Hot and Zesty Oriental Mustard (page 83)
½ teaspoon red pepper flakes
¼ cup peeled and finely shredded fresh ginger (if you have a shredding blade for your food processor, you could use it)
1½ teaspoons salt, or to taste
2 teaspoons sugar
¼ cup dry sherry
1 cup peanut or vegetable oil
1 to 2 cups firmly packed chopped cilantro (fresh coriander), the amount depending on how much you like the flavor

Dhal with Mustard Seeds and Ginger

¼ cup vegetable oil

1 tablespoon black or brown mustard seeds

1 teaspoon cumin seeds

1 teaspoon red pepper flakes

1 teaspoon peeled and shredded fresh
ginger

3 cloves garlic, finely minced

¼ teaspoon coarsely ground black
pepper

1½ cups dried red lentils, picked
over, rinsed, and drained

½ teaspoon turmeric

4½ cups water

1 teaspoon salt

1 large yellow onion, thinly sliced,
with rings separated

About 1 cup plain yogurt

Finally, just barely beyond the Pacific Rim, from India—the place, most historians agree, where mustard first found its way into the kitchen—I bring you one last dish: dhal. *Dhal* is the Indian word for lentils, which are traditionally served with a garnishing of sliced onions, fried to a golden brown, and a dollop of plain yogurt. In most Indian dishes, mustard seeds are used whole. But don't worry, when they're cooked in this manner, the potency is greatly tamed. Boiled rice and a selection of Indian breads would more than complete the meal.

Heat 3 tablespoons of the oil in a large, heavy pan over medium-high heat. Add the mustard seeds, cumin, red pepper, ginger, garlic, and black pepper and cook, stirring, for about 60 seconds. Stir in the lentils and turmeric and heat for another minute or so, then add the water and salt. Cover the pan and simmer gently over medium heat until the lentils are soft and tender, 35 to 45 minutes.

When the lentils are almost finished cooking, heat the remaining tablespoon of oil in a medium-size skillet over medium to medium-high heat. Add the onion and cook, stirring, until the onion is translucent and lightly golden.

Garnish each serving of dhal with a portion of the sautéed onions and a dollop of yogurt. Dhal also makes a lovely accompaniment to roast chicken.

Makes 6 to 8 servings.

Chapter Five

American Mustards—
A Regional Celebration

In typical American style, we have adopted and adapted the mustards of the world. We love a hot and grainy Louisiana-style mustard, expect a Southwest mustard to be laced with fiery bits of chile and cumin, and bat nary an eye (on the California scene, at least) at the thought of raspberry mustard.

Admittedly, it took us a while to get to this point. Until Francis French acted on his hunch that the American palate simply wasn't ready for sophisticated European mustards and created a toned-down offering, we didn't hold the condiment in very high regard.

Ultimately, however, the good old mellow-yellow style of mustard he introduced gained such a foothold in the American kitchen—not to mention every ballpark from New York to L.A.—that most of us weren't open to variations beyond a select few identified with our home region. It's only been in the last decade that specialty mustards have taken off. Now there are hundreds of brands available from large and small producers right here in the United States.

WEST COAST

People in the West lean toward a hot-sweet mustard, which complements their lighter style of cooking. California gourmets are looking for simple, delectable spreads that will zip up an unassuming entrée of grilled fillet of snapper or poached breast of chicken. They seek flavorings that can be whisked into delicate vinaigrettes to accompany a fresh platter of salad greens; condiments that, when spread on a toasted onion bagel, will harmonize with smoked salmon and cream cheese.

Dijon-style varieties laced with herbs and fruit purees or citrus peel are velvety in texture, with an intense flavor that admirably partners with many West Coast cheese, game, and poultry dishes.

Honey mustards, some of which supposedly owe their character to the source of the nectar used to make the honey—thyme, wildflowers, lavender, etc.—are also popular. In truth, though, it matters little whether the honey comes from bees obsessed with orange blossoms or clover. Once it is blended into a batch of fiery mustard, the botanic subtleties are lost. Better to spend your time and money tracking down the finest herbs and mustard seeds you can find. Spring for the well-aged bottle of balsamic vinegar and the vintage Napa Valley Sauvignon Blanc. It's the proper selection and blending of these components that will make or break your creation.

Honey Mustard of Lime and Celery Seeds with Balsamic Vinegar

½ cup yellow mustard seeds
¾ cup balsamic vinegar
¼ cup water
2 teaspoons celery seeds
1 teaspoon coriander seeds
2 tablespoons honey
2 teaspoons salt
1 tablespoon finely grated lime rind
2 to 3 tablespoons fresh lime juice

This is definitely a West Coast kind of condiment, nicely balanced between citrus and mustard, with sweet coriander and balsamic vinegar overtones. Try whisking a bit into a light vinaigrette of oil and vinegar for a smashing accompaniment to a fresh salad of mixed greens.

In a nonaluminum pot or jar, combine the mustard seeds, vinegar, water, and celery and coriander seeds; cover and soak for 48 hours, adding additional vinegar if necessary to maintain enough liquid to cover the seeds.

Scrape the soaked seeds into a food processor. Add the remaining ingredients and process until the mustard turns from liquid and seeds to a creamy mixture flecked with seeds. This takes 3 to 4 minutes. Add additional vinegar as necessary to create a nice creamy mustard; keep in mind that it will thicken slightly upon standing. This mustard can be used immediately.

Makes about 1 ½ cups.

California Mustard of Sun-dried Tomatoes and Basil

This has a beautiful, rich, golden-red color and is exquisitely flavored with sun-dried tomatoes and herbs. For a mustard, it's unexpectedly mild, yet zestfully infused with tomato, basil, and garlic. Make plenty, because as gifts go, this one will be a major hit with every foodie you know.

¾ cup yellow mustard seeds
1 cup cider vinegar
3 cloves garlic, chopped
1 cup oil-packed sun-dried tomatoes, drained and chopped
1 tablespoon dried basil, crumbled
2 teaspoons salt

In a nonaluminum pot or jar, combine the mustard seeds, vinegar, and garlic; cover and soak for 48 hours, adding additional vinegar if necessary to maintain enough liquid to cover the seeds.

Scrape the soaked seeds into a food processor. Add the remaining ingredients and process until the mustard turns from liquid and seeds to a creamy mixture flecked with seeds. The tomato bits will eventually puree into a homogeneous mixture, blending splendidly with the mustard. The process takes at least 3 to 4 minutes. Add additional vinegar as necessary to create a nice creamy mustard; keep in mind that it will thicken slightly upon standing. This mustard can be consumed immediately.

Makes 3 cups.

Pacific Northwest Whole-Grain Mustard with Horseradish

⅔ cup yellow mustard seeds
½ cup brown mustard seeds
1½ cups cider vinegar
2 cloves garlic, minced
2 to 3 teaspoons prepared horseradish
2 teaspoons salt
1 teaspoon sugar
1 teaspoon turmeric

To match the heartier, earthier cuisine so often associated with the Pacific Northwest, a zesty, heavy-textured mustard is in order. A whole-grain German style fills the bill when spiked with some of the country's best horseradish from Tule Lake in northern California. It all adds up to a walloping big taste particularly suited to high-country fare. A backpacker's delight, if you will, rich and lively enough to energize any five-day hike through the Cascades. Of course, it's equally delicious with picnic fare, from a simple repast of salami, cheese, and French bread.

In a nonaluminum pot or jar, combine the mustard seeds, vinegar, and garlic; cover and soak for 48 hours, adding additional vinegar if necessary to maintain enough liquid to cover the seeds.

Scrape the soaked seeds into a food processor. Add the remaining ingredients and process until the mustard turns from liquid and seeds to a creamy mixture flecked with seeds. This takes 3 to 4 minutes. Add additional vinegar as necessary to create a nice creamy mustard; keep in mind that it will thicken slightly upon standing. This mustard benefits from at least a week of aging.

Makes 2¾ cups.

Raspberry Mustard

You'll be surprised at the true raspberry flavor that shines through in this mustard. Of course, for the uninitiated, the real shock is that the combination works as well as it does—not on ballpark franks, to be certain, but it's definitely a condiment you'll be presenting alongside a fine honey-baked ham or a cream cheese and turkey sandwich.

In a nonaluminum pot or jar, combine the mustard seeds, vinegar, and water; cover and soak for 48 hours, adding additional vinegar and water (in the correct proportions) if necessary to maintain enough liquid to cover the seeds.

Scrape the soaked seeds into a food processor. Add the remaining ingredients and process until the mustard turns from liquid and seeds to a creamy mixture flecked with seeds. This takes 3 to 4 minutes. Add additional vinegar and water (in the correct proportions) as necessary to create a nice creamy mustard; keep in mind that it will thicken slightly upon standing. This mustard can be consumed immediately.

Makes about 2½ cups.

¾ cup yellow mustard seeds
1 cup plus 2 tablespoons raspberry vinegar
⅓ cup water
2 tablespoons honey
2 tablespoons good-quality raspberry jam
2 teaspoons salt

Note: For a smooth-textured mustard, press the mustard through a fine sieve. (The yield will be reduced to about 1½ cups.)

Without some sort of coloring additive, this mustard has a bit of a grayish yellow cast, not at all what you visualize when you think of raspberries. To make it look as appetizing as it tastes, the addition of a spoonful of beet powder, first stirred with a little water to make a paste, does the trick. You probably didn't even know you could obtain beets in powdered form (it became popular when red dye #2 came under fire), but you can, and it's the most natural and effective coloring

I've been able to find. Because a little bit goes a long way, beet powder will not affect the flavor of your mustard. Unfortunately, it isn't something your corner market is likely to carry. So please check Sources at the end of this book.

An alternate choice, of course, is plain, everyday red food coloring.

1 cup yellow mustard seeds
½ cup brown mustard seeds
1½ cups Pinot Noir (a full-bodied, dry red wine)
½ cup red wine vinegar
½ cup water
3 cloves garlic, minced
1 tablespoon dried chervil, crumbled
2 teaspoons paprika
2 teaspoons ground allspice
½ teaspoon freshly ground black pepper
½ teaspoon ground cloves
½ teaspoon turmeric
½ teaspoon ground ginger
½ teaspoon ground nutmeg
½ teaspoon dried thyme, crumbled
5 tablespoons honey

Whole-Grain Honey Mustard with Pinot Noir

This is a mustard designed to stand up to hearty fare. It's chunky in character, bold and spicy in taste, and simply beguiling in the company of grilled kielbasa.

In a nonaluminum pot or jar, combine all the ingredients except the honey; cover and soak for 48 hours, adding additional vinegar and water (in the correct proportions) if necessary to maintain enough liquid to cover the seeds.

Scrape half of the mixture into a food processor. Process until the mustard turns from liquid and seeds to a creamy mixture flecked with seeds. This takes 3 to 4 minutes. Add additional vinegar and water (in the correct proportions) as necessary to create a nice creamy mustard. Scrape this mixture into a bowl and combine with the remaining whole-seeds mixture. Stir in the honey. This mustard benefits from 2 to 3 weeks of aging.

Makes about 3⅓ cups.

East Meets West Mustard

⚜

⅔ cup yellow mustard seeds
½ cup brown mustard seeds
1½ cups rice vinegar
½ cup water
3 cloves garlic, minced
¼ cup sesame seeds, toasted (see note on page 78)
3 tablespoons peeled and finely grated fresh ginger
1 tablespoon sesame oil (see note on page 78)
2 teaspoons salt
1 teaspoon sugar

This mustard makes a bold, delectable statement. Redolent of fresh ginger and toasted sesame seeds with a garlicky backdrop, it is a canary yellow color, accented by the whole brown seeds.

In a nonaluminum pot or jar, combine the mustard seeds, vinegar, water, and garlic; cover and soak for 48 hours, adding additional vinegar and water (in the correct proportions) if necessary to maintain enough liquid to cover the seeds.

Scrape the soaked seeds into a food processor. Add the remaining ingredients and process until the mustard turns from liquid and seeds to a creamy mixture flecked with seeds. This takes 3 to 4 minutes. Add additional vinegar and water (in the correct proportions) as necessary to create a nice creamy mustard; keep in mind that it will thicken slightly upon standing. This mustard benefits from 2 to 3 weeks of aging.

Makes about 3¾ cups.

Cabbage Salad with Green Peppers and Sun-dried Tomatoes

An extremely flavorful salad.

Combine the cabbage with the bell pepper and tomatoes. Toss with some of the vinaigrette, season with black pepper, toss again, and adjust the seasonings. If possible, refrigerate the salad for about 30 minutes to develop the flavors. May be made several hours ahead.

Makes about 8 servings.

6 cups finely shredded green cabbage

1 large green bell pepper, seeded and finely chopped or cut into thin strips

½ cup oil-packed sun-dried tomatoes, drained and chopped

California Vinaigrette (recipe follows)

Freshly ground black pepper to taste

California Vinaigrette

Combine all the ingredients except the oils in a small bowl with a wire whisk. Continue whisking as you slowly pour in the oils; adjust the seasonings. This will keep in the refrigerator for about 2 weeks.

Makes 1¼ cups.

½ cup red wine vinegar

2 tablespoons California Mustard of Sun-dried Tomatoes and Basil (see page 101)

½ teaspoon salt

1¼ teaspoons sugar

¼ cup extra virgin olive oil, or the oil from the sun-dried tomatoes used to make the mustard, or a mixture of the two

½ cup vegetable oil

2 or 3 slices bacon, diced

1 small red onion, diced

1 tablespoon chopped shallots

2 cloves garlic, minced

1 cup fresh black-eyed peas, blanched in boiling water until tender, about 7 minutes (see note on page 109)

½ teaspoon dried thyme, crumbled

½ cup extra virgin olive oil

¼ cup Champagne or white wine vinegar

Pinch of ground cayenne pepper

1 tablespoon California Mustard of Sun-dried Tomatoes and Basil (see page 101) or Honey Mustard of Lime and Celery Seeds with Balsamic Vinegar (page 100)

½ cup tomato concasse (see note on page 109)

½ cup chopped scallions, both green and white parts

Salt and freshly ground black pepper to taste

Twelve 1-ounce, ⅛-inch-thick slices cold rare roasted leg of lamb

About 4 or 5 cups bite-size pieces frisée (see note on page 109)

Warm Lamb and Black-Eyed Pea Salad in Mustard Vinaigrette

From the moment we stepped into Cafe Roti, just off the lobby of the Hotel Griffon, with its sweeping view of San Francisco Bay, I felt comfortable and pampered. Elegance and Old San Francisco charm oozed from the polished woodwork, the crisp white linen, and the sparkling crystal. From custom-designed rotisseries inside the huge fireplace in the main dining room the cooking staff produces its California Cuisine specialties: roasted beef, lamb, and fowl. In order to sample some, I ordered the warm lamb and black-eyed pea salad, which turned out to be an exceptionally well-thought-out blending of flavors, textures, and colors. It is a gentle contrast in taste and appearance achieved with velvety-tender, paper-thin slices of warm lamb juxtaposed with crisp, tart leaves of frisée, black-eyed peas, and tomato concasse in vinaigrette.

I have adapted Chef Manuel Goodman's original recipe so that it can stand up to the mustard vinaigrette I created for this book. Use only the finest-quality lamb and the freshest of greens.

Cook the bacon gently over medium heat to render the fat, then add the onions, shallots, and garlic and continue cooking to allow the flavors to blend, about 5 minutes. Add the peas, thyme, olive oil, vinegar, and cayenne. Cook for 3 minutes, then reduce the heat to low and add the mustard, tomatoes, scallions, salt, and pepper. Keep warm.

Arrange 3 slices of lamb on each plate. Warm slightly in a preheated 250°F oven. In a large bowl, toss the black-eyed pea mixture with the frisée. (The black-eyed pea mixture acts as a warm vinaigrette for the salad.) Remove the frisée from the bowl and place in the center of each

plate. Sprinkle any remaining pea mixture over the frisée and lamb. Drizzle the remaining vinaigrette over the plates and serve immediately.
Makes 4 servings.

Note: Fresh black-eyed peas are the best, but dried or frozen peas can be used. Cook by following package directions.

The word *concasse* comes from the French *concasser*, meaning to coarsely chop food with a knife. It refers, in this case, to peeled and seeded tomatoes that are cut into small dice.

Frisée, or curly endive, has become a popular salad green in recent years, a "designer green," if you will. The light green leaves are tangy yet sweet in flavor, somewhat spiky in appearance, and fairly firm textured—which means they can stand up to a warm dressing. If unavailable in your area, I suggest a mixed collection of baby dandelion greens (or very tender mature dandelion greens), arugula, radicchio, and escarole.

Cucumbers and Tomatoes in Mustard Dressing

¼ cup rice vinegar

2 tablespoons Whole-Grain Honey Mustard with Pinot Noir (see page 104) or East Meets West Mustard (page 106)

⅓ cup extra virgin olive oil

2 tablespoons minced fresh chives

¼ teaspoon salt, or to taste

Freshly ground black pepper to taste

4 medium-size cucumbers, peeled and thinly sliced

About 1½ cups cherry tomatoes (if larger than ½ inch in diameter, cut in half)

Use local summer produce for the best flavor and a lovely pottery bowl for a smashing presentation.

Whisk together the vinegar and mustard, then whisk in the olive oil in a steady stream. Add the chives, salt, and pepper. Pour the dressing over the cucumbers and allow the mixture to marinate for several hours or overnight in the refrigerator. Just before serving, add the tomatoes and toss to coat well.

Makes 6 to 8 servings.

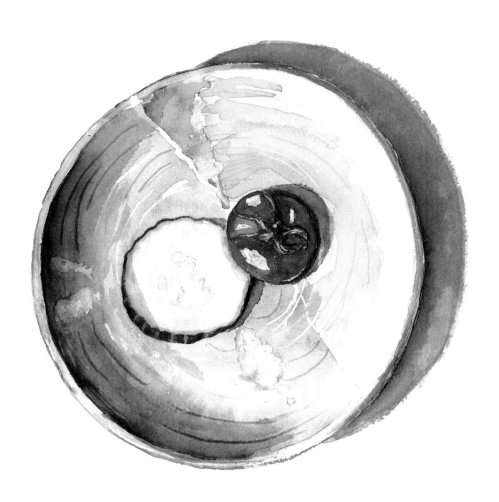

American Mustards

California Quiche

4 large eggs

¾ cup sour cream

¼ to ½ teaspoon salt

⅓ cup California Mustard of Sun-dried Tomatoes and Basil (see page 101)

One unbaked 9-inch pie shell

2 tablespoons butter

1 large onion, diced

2 cups sliced mushrooms

Chopped fresh dill, additional salt, and freshly ground black pepper to taste

2 cups shredded zucchini

2 cups shredded fine-quality Swiss cheese

1 cup peeled, seeded, and diced tomatoes

¼ cup chopped black olives

One of my favorite mustards—the California Mustard of Sun-dried Tomatoes and Basil—is spread over the bottom crust of this quiche before the creamy filling is poured in. That thin, zesty inner layer gives a wonderful piquancy to the dish.

Beat the eggs with the sour cream and the ¼ to ½ teaspoon salt until well blended; set aside. Spread the mustard over the bottom of the pie shell; set aside.

Melt the butter in a large saucepan over medium heat. Add the onion, mushrooms, dill, additional salt, and pepper and cook, stirring, until the onion is soft and translucent and the mushrooms lightly browned. Meanwhile, place the zucchini in a sieve and press out as much moisture as possible. Spread the zucchini and the mushroom mixture over the bottom of the pie shell, sprinkle on half the cheese, then pour on the egg and sour cream mixture. Add the tomatoes and olives and spread the remaining cheese on top. Bake in a preheated 350°F oven until set and golden, 30 to 45 minutes.

Makes one 9-inch quiche; 6 servings.

American Mustards

2 slices *fine-quality seven-grain bread, thickly sliced, if possible*
2 to 3 tablespoons *(a generous slab!) cream cheese, at room temperature*
1 or 2 slices *fine-quality ham*
2 thick slices *vine-ripened tomato*
Several *paper-thin slices ice-crisp cucumber*
Several *paper-thin slices red onion*
Small *handful alfalfa sprouts*
Generous *slathering of Raspberry Mustard (see page 103)*

Ham, Cream Cheese, Tomatoes, and Sprouts on Toasted Seven-Grain Bread with Red Raspberry Mustard

If you're trying to be good, bypass the real cream cheese and opt for one of the reduced-fat or fat-free substitutes.

Thoroughly toast both sides of the bread, either in a toaster or under the broiler. To build your sandwich, first spread the cream cheese on one of the bread slices. Top with the ham, tomato, cucumber, and onion, then crown it with a sprinkling of sprouts. Spread a bit of mustard on the second slice of bread before capping the masterpiece.

Makes 1 sandwich.

1¼ pounds *white or red boiling potatoes*
⅓ cup *Whole-Grain Honey Mustard with Pinot Noir (see page 104) or East Meets West Mustard (page 106)*
⅓ cup *white wine or cider vinegar*
⅓ cup *vegetable oil*
½ teaspoon *salt*
1 cup *chopped scallions, both green and white parts*

Potato Salad with Honey Pinot Mustard

This is a delicious but basic salad that easily can be zipped up with your favorite potato salad ingredients—hard-cooked egg, cucumber, crisp bits of real bacon, and pickles.

Place the potatoes in a large pot with water to cover. Bring to a boil and simmer over medium heat until the potatoes are tender, about 20 minutes, depending on the size. Remove from the heat, drain, and cool slightly until the potatoes can be handled. Peel and cut into chunks. In a small bowl, combine the mustard, vinegar, oil, salt, and scallions.

Toss the dressing with the potatoes, then chill for at least 1 hour, or up to 24 hours, before serving.

Makes about 6 servings.

Honey Mustard Vinaigrette

Because of its innate thickening power and intense flavor, mustard is a wonderful addition to a basic vinaigrette.

In a small bowl, whisk together the vinegar, mustard, olive oil, and chives, then add the honey and mix again until thoroughly blended. This vinaigrette will keep for about 2 weeks in the refrigerator.

Makes about ½ cup.

¼ cup white wine vinegar
2 tablespoons Classic Dijon (see page 20) or herbed mustard such as Pesto Mustard (page 28) or California Mustard of Sun-dried Tomatoes and Basil (page 101)
2 tablespoons extra virgin olive oil
2 tablespoons minced fresh chives
1 tablespoon honey

THE SOUTH

Southerners like their bourbon smooth and smoky, and their mustards hot and spicy. So it should come as no surprise that the best-known Southern mustards come from Louisiana, mother of two of the nation's most popular—and spicy—cuisines: Creole and Cajun.

A true Louisiana-style mustard incorporates some of the region's most distinctive flavorings: bay leaves from the laurel tree, and, for kick, an abundance of different peppers, such as cayenne and Tabasco. Other ingredients—sherry, green peppercorns, herbs—provide a depth that Creole and Cajun specialties just can't do without. Lest you suspect that association with such well-defined cuisines restricts improvisation, consider that a sweet and aromatic orange honey mustard has been all the rage in the region since the late eighties.

Louisiana Mustard

¾ cup yellow mustard seeds
½ cup distilled vinegar
½ cup dry sherry
1 tablespoon green peppercorns,
    drained and rinsed
2 cloves garlic, minced
2 to 3 teaspoons Louisiana Spice
    Mix (recipe follows)

A combination of such Louisiana specialties as cayenne pepper, peppercorns, garlic, paprika, and oregano contributes to this mustard's distinctive style and flavor.

In a nonaluminum pot or jar, combine the mustard seeds, vinegar, sherry, peppercorns, and garlic; cover and soak for 48 hours, adding additional vinegar and sherry (in equal amounts) if necessary to maintain enough liquid to cover the seeds.

Scrape the soaked seeds into a food processor. Add the Louisiana spice mix and process until the mustard turns from liquid and seeds to a creamy mixture flecked with seeds. This takes 3 to 4 minutes. Add additional vinegar and sherry (in equal amounts) as necessary to create a nice creamy mustard; keep in mind that it will thicken upon standing. This mustard can be consumed immediately.

Makes 2 cups.

Louisiana Spice Mix

Combine all of the ingredients. This will keep for several months if stored in a cool, dry place in an airtight container.

Makes about ½ cup.

2 tablespoons ground cayenne pepper
2 tablespoons salt
4 teaspoons sweet Hungarian paprika
4 teaspoons freshly ground black pepper
4 teaspoons garlic powder
2 teaspoons ground white pepper
2 teaspoons dried thyme, crumbled
2 teaspoons dried oregano, crumbled

Georgia Peach and Bourbon Mustard Dijon Style

A rather hot and sweet mustard that has a definite affinity for meat. Besides using it in the recipe for ribs on page 122, you might also use this mustard in a glaze for your next baked ham; just combine equal parts of the mustard, firmly packed brown sugar, peach jam, and dry sherry.

After the mustard has been pressed through the sieve, stir in the peach jam and puree once again in the food processor. This mustard can be consumed immediately.

Makes 1½ scant cups.

1 recipe Classic Dijon (see page 20, and read these instructions first), substituting ¼ cup bourbon for the white wine
¼ cup peach jam

Orange Honey Cream Mustard

¼ cup yellow mustard seeds
¾ cup cider vinegar
¼ cup rum
1½ tablespoons honey
1½ tablespoons coconut cream
   (available in the liquor-supply
   section of the supermarket)
1¼ teaspoons salt
One very tiny drop (from a toothpick) orange oil (see note below)

This is the mustard that's been such a rage. I took a few liberties by adding just a splash of rum and a hint of coconut cream. Blend a spoonful into about a quarter cup of heavy cream, and you've got a quick sauce for grilled pork.

In a nonaluminum pot or jar, combine the mustard seeds, vinegar, and rum; cover and soak for 48 hours, adding additional vinegar and rum (in the correct proportions) if necessary to maintain enough liquid to cover the seeds.

Scrape the soaked seeds into a food processor. Add the honey, coconut cream, salt, and orange oil and process until the mustard turns from liquid and seeds to a creamy mixture flecked with seeds. This takes 3 to 4 minutes. Add additional vinegar and rum (in the correct proportions) as necessary to create a nice creamy mustard; keep in mind that it will thicken slightly upon standing. This mustard can be consumed immediately.

Makes about 2⅓ cups.

Note: Orange oil is a *very* concentrated substance, so a drop from a toothpick is all you need. It is very different from orange extract. If you can't locate it in your area, check the Sources section at the back of this book, where I've recommended a high-quality, nonbitter brand made by Boyajian.

Celeriac Remoulade

This is a popular northern European first course that crossed the Atlantic and became a hit in New Orleans. It's a lovely salad when you combine the perfectly julienned, creamy-white, and crunchy raw celeriac with the classic remoulade dressing and serve it next to grated carrots and beets and sliced tomatoes.

With a sharp knife, peel the celeriac and cut into 1- to 1½-inch-long julienne strips to measure 4 cups. Place the slices in acidulated water (water and lemon juice) as you go to prevent darkening.

To prepare the remoulade dressing, whisk together the remaining ingredients, except the garnishes, until smooth. The dressing may be prepared and refrigerated up to 24 hours ahead.

Drain the celeriac well and combine with the remoulade. Marinate in the refrigerator for 2 hours before serving. Arrange on individual salad plates, alongside the shredded carrots and beets and the sliced tomatoes.

Makes 6 servings.

1 whole celeriac

1 cup mayonnaise

3 tablespoons Louisiana Mustard (see page 116)

3 tablespoons finely chopped scallions, the white part and some of the green

2 tablespoons minced fresh parsley

1 tablespoon drained and rinsed capers, finely chopped

1 tablespoon finely chopped cornichons (if unavailable, baby garlic dills may be substituted)

1 tablespoon finely minced sweet pickles

1 teaspoon fresh lemon juice

½ teaspoon dried tarragon, crumbled

½ teaspoon dried chervil, crumbled

½ teaspoon anchovy paste

For accompanying garnish, if desired: grated carrots and beets, and sliced tomatoes

Louisiana Beer Shrimp with Mustard Dipping Sauce

4 dozen medium-size shrimp (about 2 pounds)

5 teaspoons Louisiana Spice Mix (see page 117)

2 large eggs

1¾ cups all-purpose flour

½ cup beer

¼ cup water

1 tablespoon baking powder

¼ teaspoon salt

3 cups unsweetened flaked coconut

Vegetable oil for deep frying

Mustard Dipping Sauce (recipe follows)

Coconut and shrimp are a popular combination in this region of the country. Be sure that you use unsweetened coconut or the flavor will be unbalanced. If you're short on time (and spices), instead of preparing your own Louisiana spice mix, buy one of the many commercial products on the market.

Prepare the shrimp by peeling all but the tails and deveining them; set aside. Combine 1 tablespoon of the Louisiana spice mix with the eggs, 1¼ cups of the flour, the beer, water, baking powder, and salt; mix well to make sure there are no lumps (this can be done in a food processor).

In another bowl, combine the remaining flour and spice mix; set aside. Place the coconut in a third bowl.

Holding the shrimp by the tail, dredge them in the dry flour mixture, shaking off the excess, then dip them in batter up to, but not covering, the tail. Let the excess drip off, then coat generously with the grated coconut and place on a baking pan.

Meanwhile, heat 3 inches of oil in a deep fryer to 350°F. Test the temperature by shaking a small drop of batter into the oil. If it sizzles and turns golden within about 10 seconds, the oil is hot enough. Drop the shrimp into the oil one by one, cooking only a few at a time so the temperature of the oil doesn't drop. Fry the shrimp in several batches until golden brown, 30 seconds to 1 minute per side. Drain on paper towels. Serve immediately with the dipping sauce.

Makes 12 appetizer servings, or 6 entrée servings.

Mustard Dipping Sauce

⁂

Combine all of the ingredients. This sauce will keep in the refrigerator for many months.

Makes about 2½ cups.

⅓ cup Orange Honey Cream Mustard (see page 118)

⅓ cup prepared horseradish (for a slightly milder sauce, use a cream-style horseradish)

1½ cups orange marmalade

¼ cup prepared chili sauce (look for it in your supermarket next to the ketchup)

1 cup cider vinegar

1 cup dry red wine

½ cup ketchup

¼ cup (½ stick) butter or margarine

2 cups finely minced onion

2 tablespoons peach jam

1 tablespoon Georgia Peach and Bourbon Mustard Dijon Style (see page 117)

1 tablespoon Worcestershire sauce

2 cloves garlic, minced

1 teaspoon salt

1 teaspoon hot paprika

About 6 pounds beef spareribs (figure 4 or 5 ribs per person)

Oven-Barbecued Ribs

Thanks to the generous addition of Georgia Peach and Bourbon Mustard, these ribs are quite zesty. If you'd like to add a bit of down-home smoke to the flavor, finish the ribs over a grill during the last 30 minutes of cooking. But keep a squirt bottle of water handy, because the sauce will really kick up the flames.

Combine all the ingredients except the ribs in a medium-size saucepan and bring to a boil over medium-high heat. Reduce the heat to medium-low and simmer about 10 minutes; remove from the heat and let cool.

Pour the cooled marinade over the ribs, cover, and refrigerate for 6 hours or overnight, turning occasionally to thoroughly coat the ribs.

Remove the ribs from the marinade and place in a roasting pan; roast in a preheated 325°F oven for 1½ hours, turning and basting occasionally with the marinade.

Makes 6 servings.

THE SOUTHWEST

Few styles of American cooking have such wide appeal as that of the Southwest. Perhaps this is because it is both one of the newest and, in many ways, one of the fastest-evolving styles. There's a commonality of ingredients and presentation that unifies all Mexican-American cooking, but depending on the state, or even the city, interpretations are extravagantly diverse. An enchilada in Santa Fe may have all the markings of a Texas soft-shell taco. Some Southwest cooks wouldn't dream of leaving beans out of their chili con carne, while others consider their inclusion a form of culinary travesty. There can be endless discussions of cumin versus oregano, longhorn cheddar versus Monterey Jack, dried and ground chiles versus fresh, and ground versus shredded beef.

So where do mustards fit into the picture? Well, it would be an overstatement to say they are central to southwestern cooking. But nothing as adaptable as mustard need be far from the action. For example, in my favorite southwestern-style restaurant, Bombs Away Cafe—which also happens to be one of the best in the Pacific Northwest—chef John Huyck uses mustards in a variety of ways. Because of its marvelous thickening ability, mustard is often present in the cafe's vinaigrettes. Huyck also creates a flavorful sauce for one of his fish specialties by combining whole-grain mustard, chopped cilantro, avocado, and heavy cream. Another quick sauce of which he's particularly fond incorporates whole-grain mustard with heavy cream, cilantro, and crabmeat. Although such a blending would complement any number of poultry offerings, Huyck says he devised it to pour over diamond-shaped servings of firm polenta. Garnished with lime and a fan of sliced avocado, it is quite a spectacular dish.

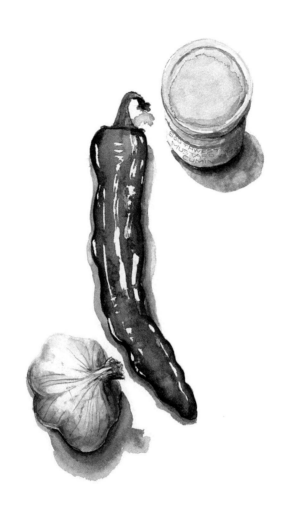

Jalapeño Mustard

This is a much hotter version of the Southwest Chile Mustard with Cumin. Remember, the brown and black mustard seeds have a more potent flavor than the yellow. This recipe can be slightly tamed by substituting the lighter-colored seeds.

In a nonaluminum pot or jar, combine the mustard seeds, vinegar, wine, pimientos, chiles, red pepper flakes, jalapeño, and garlic; cover and soak for 48 hours, adding additional vinegar and wine (in the correct proportions) if necessary to maintain enough liquid to cover the seeds.

Scrape the soaked seeds into a food processor. Add the remaining ingredients and process until the mustard turns from liquid and seeds to a creamy mixture flecked with seeds. This takes 3 to 4 minutes. Add additional vinegar and wine (in the correct proportions) as necessary to create a nice creamy mustard; keep in mind that it will thicken slightly upon standing. This mustard benefits from about 2 weeks of aging.

Makes 3 scant cups.

¾ cup brown mustard seeds
¾ cup cider vinegar
½ cup dry white wine
2 tablespoons diced pimientos
1 tablespoon canned diced chiles
2 teaspoons red pepper flakes
1 jalapeño pepper, seeded and minced
3 cloves garlic, chopped
2 teaspoons ground cumin
1 teaspoon dried oregano, crumbled
1 teaspoon hot pepper sauce
1 teaspoon salt

Southwest Chile Mustard with Cumin

½ cup brown mustard seeds
¼ cup yellow mustard seeds
¾ cup red wine vinegar
½ cup beer
2 teaspoons red pepper flakes
3 cloves garlic, chopped
1 tablespoon ground cumin
2 teaspoons celery salt
1 teaspoon hot pepper sauce

This mustard takes very little getting used to. Most fall instantly in love with its rich cumin-garlic flavor. The creamy version is particularly tantalizing.

In a nonaluminum pot or jar, combine the mustard seeds, vinegar, beer, red pepper flakes, and garlic; cover and soak for 48 hours, adding additional vinegar and beer (in the correct proportions) if necessary to maintain enough liquid to cover the seeds.

Scrape the soaked seeds into a food processor. Add the cumin, celery salt, and hot pepper sauce and process until the mustard turns from liquid and seeds to a creamy mixture flecked with seeds. This takes 3 to 4 minutes. Add additional vinegar and beer (in the correct proportions) as necessary to create a nice creamy mustard; keep in mind that it will thicken slightly upon standing. Although this mustard is smashing from the moment it emerges from the food processor, a week or so of aging does improve it even more.

Makes 2¾ cups.

Creamy version: For a scrumptiously smooth mustard, press through a medium- to fine-mesh wire sieve using a rubber spatula or wooden spoon. Makes about 1½ cups.

Roasted Sweet Red Pepper Mustard
with Cumin

When I developed this recipe, my crop of golden bell peppers was not yet ready for harvesting. But once it was, I couldn't resist trying the recipe again, using the marvelous amber-toned peppers. The experiment was highly successful, so feel free to use either color.

In a nonaluminum pot or jar, combine the mustard seeds, vinegar, wine, and garlic; cover and soak in the refrigerator for 48 hours, adding additional vinegar and wine (in equal amounts) if necessary to maintain enough liquid to cover the seeds.

Scrape the soaked seeds into a food processor. Add the remaining ingredients and process until the pepper is almost completely pureed (there will still be tiny flecks and chunks) and the mustard has become fairly creamy but still contains quite a few whole mustard seeds. The process will take no more than 2 or 3 minutes. Don't worry if you overprocess the mixture. Your mustard will simply have a smoother texture. Add additional vinegar and wine (in equal amounts) as necessary to create a nice creamy mustard; keep in mind that it will thicken slightly upon standing. This mustard can be consumed immediately.

Makes 3½ cups.

Note: To roast and peel a pepper, pierce it with a sharp knife (to prevent bursting), then roast either under the broiler or on a grill, turning as each side blisters. The extra flavor imparted by a grill makes it the best choice, if available. Place the hot roasted pepper in a plastic bag and put it in the freezer for 10 minutes so the steam can loosen the skin; remove from the freezer. Gently slip off the skin.

1 cup yellow mustard seeds
¾ cup cider vinegar
¾ cup dry white wine
3 cloves garlic, coarsely chopped
1 medium-size red, yellow, or golden bell pepper, roasted (see note below), peeled, seeded, and chopped
1 tablespoon chili powder
1 tablespoon ground cumin
2 teaspoons salt

Cilantro Mustard with Toasted Pine Nuts

½ cup yellow mustard seeds

3 tablespoons brown mustard seeds

1 cup cider vinegar

¼ cup water

½ cup firmly packed chopped cilantro (fresh coriander)

3 cloves garlic, coarsely chopped

½ cup pine nuts, toasted (see note
on page 43)

2 teaspoons salt

1 teaspoon dried oregano, crumbled

If you're fond of cilantro, then you will be happy with this recipe. The strong flavor of this trendy herb is not lost in the mustard. Nor, sur-prisingly enough, is the toasty flavor of the pine nuts.

In a nonaluminum pot or jar, combine the mustard seeds, vinegar, water, cilantro, and garlic; cover and soak for 48 hours, adding additional vinegar and water (in the correct proportions) if necessary to maintain enough liquid to cover the seeds.

Scrape the soaked seeds into a food processor. Add the remaining ingredients, then process until the mustard turns from liquid and seeds to a creamy mixture flecked with seeds. The pine nuts will eventually puree into a homogeneous mixture, blending splendidly with the mus-tard. The process takes at least 3 to 4 minutes. Add additional vinegar and water (in the correct proportions) if necessary to create a nice creamy mustard; keep in mind that it will thicken slightly upon standing. A bit of aging, only 2 to 3 weeks, seems to bring out the cilantro and pine nut flavors.

Makes about 2 cups.

Grilled Pickled Pepper Sandwich

In this recipe chiles are roasted, peeled, and pickled, then tossed with a mountain of shredded cheese. Grill the combo on hearty slices of whole-grain bread, slathered with a cumin-laced chile mustard.

Lay the roasted and peeled chiles out in a single layer in a plastic container with a flat bottom.

In a saucepan, combine the vinegar, oil, cumin seeds, garlic, sugar, and salt; bring to a boil and simmer over medium heat for 10 minutes; remove from the heat and allow to cool about 5 minutes. Pour the marinade through a strainer over the chiles, cover well, and refrigerate at least 8 hours. The chiles can be refrigerated for up to 1 week before use.

When ready to serve, spread one side of each slice of bread with a generous amount of the mustard. Lift the chiles from the marinade, drain well, then cut into thin strips. If you want a little less fire, remove the seeds. Toss the chile strips with the shredded cheese, then divide the cheese mixture evenly among 4 slices of the bread. Top with a second slice. Heat the butter on a griddle or in a large skillet over medium heat. Grill the sandwiches until lightly golden on one side, then flip and grill on the other side until it is golden and the cheese has melted.

Makes 4 sandwiches.

4 Anaheim chiles, each one measuring 5 or 6 inches long, roasted (see note on page 127) and peeled

1 cup red or white wine vinegar

¼ cup vegetable oil

2 teaspoons cumin seeds

1 clove garlic, peeled and slightly crushed

1 teaspoon sugar

½ teaspoon salt

8 slices fine-quality whole-grain bread

Southwest Chile Mustard with Cumin (see page 126)

3 cups shredded Monterey Jack cheese

About 2 teaspoons butter or oil

3 medium-size red bell peppers, roasted (see note on page 127) and peeled

2 Anaheim or poblano chiles (if either one is unavailable, use green bell peppers), roasted (see note on page 127) and peeled

½ head romaine lettuce, torn into bite-size pieces

1½ cups Pickled Yellow Squash (recipe follows)

8 ounces feta cheese, crumbled

½ cup pine nuts, lightly toasted (see note on page 43)

Southwest Mustard Vinaigrette (see page 131)

Roasted Red Pepper Salad with Pickled Yellow Squash

A wonderful combination of flavors and colors.

Cut the roasted chiles into long, narrow strips. Remove the seeds. In a large salad bowl, combine the lettuce, pickled squash, feta cheese, and pine nuts. Add enough of the vinaigrette to evenly coat the ingredients, and gently toss. Distribute the mixture among 6 salad plates. Arrange the roasted peppers on top of the salads, drizzle on a bit of additional vinaigrette, and serve.

Makes 6 servings.

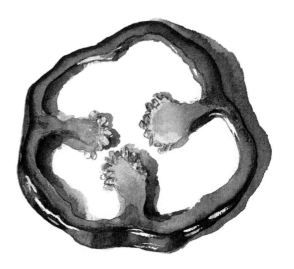

Pickled Yellow Squash

I learned from chef John Huyck, co-owner of Bombs Away Cafe, a popular Corvallis, Oregon, eatery, that pickled squash is a wonderful thing to have on hand. One of his favorite ways of using this piquant tidbit—and the first way I experienced it at the cafe—was in a chilled cream of cucumber soup. It's also delicious in three-bean salads.

Place the diced squash in a clean jar. Combine the water and vinegar and pour over the chunks. Add the mustard seeds and salt. Cap tightly and hold in the refrigerator for at least 3 days before using. It will keep for up to several weeks.

Makes about 1 quart.

1½ cups baby yellow squash cut into ¼-inch chunks, or mature yellow squash cut into ½-inch chunks

1½ cups water

1½ cups distilled vinegar

2 teaspoons yellow mustard seeds

½ teaspoon salt

Southwest Mustard Vinaigrette

In a small bowl, whisk together the vinegar, mustard, garlic, cilantro, and salt. In a slow, steady stream, pour in the oil, whisking constantly. This will keep at least 2 weeks in the refrigerator.

Makes about 1 cup.

⅓ cup white wine vinegar

1 tablespoon Southwest Chile Mustard with Cumin (see page 126)

2 cloves garlic, minced

1 to 2 teaspoons finely minced cilantro (fresh coriander)

1 teaspoon salt

⅔ cup vegetable oil (up to half could be virgin olive oil)

1 pound cooked fresh Pacific shrimp

2 cups julienned peeled jicama (the strips should measure no wider than 1/8 inch and no longer than 1 1/2 inches) or two 5-ounce cans sliced water chestnuts

1/2 cup sliced black olives

1/2 cup chopped scallions, both white and green parts

Cilantro Vinaigrette (recipe follows)

3 large tomatoes, cored and sliced

2 ripe avocados (preferably the Haas variety), peeled, pitted, and sliced

Sprigs of cilantro (fresh coriander) for garnish

Shrimp Salad with Cilantro Vinaigrette

If tiny Pacific shrimp are not available fresh, substitute the meat from fresh local cooked crab. Medium-size shrimp that have been cooked in boiling water just until opaque all the way through, peeled, and diced would also work well.

Combine the shrimp, jicama, olives, and scallions in a bowl. Add enough of the vinaigrette to evenly coat the ingredients, and gently toss. Divide the tomato and avocado slices among 4 dinner plates, arranging them in an attractive overlapping pattern. Spoon one-fourth of the shrimp mixture onto each plate, garnish with cilantro, and serve.

Makes 4 servings.

1/4 cup tarragon vinegar

2 tablespoons Cilantro Mustard with Toasted Pine Nuts (see page 128)

2 teaspoons sugar

2/3 cup vegetable oil

Salt and freshly ground black pepper to taste

Cilantro Vinaigrette

In a small bowl, whisk together the vinegar, mustard, and sugar. In a slow, steady stream, pour in the oil, whisking all the while. Adjust the flavors and season with salt and pepper. This will keep in the refrigerator for at least 2 weeks.

Makes about 1 cup.

THE NORTHEAST

In a city where the German frankfurter first officially came ashore, where soft and steamy pretzels are sold from street carts, and corned beef can be found in dozens of forms, can mustard be far from a diner's reach? Indeed not. New Yorkers love their mustard. Be it a ballpark variety that complements a Coney Island dog, or one of the spicy whole-grain German or Polish styles that stand up to a platter of sauerkraut and steamed sausages, you'll find it there.

But passions for this adaptable condiment aren't confined to New York gourmands. Mustard manufacturers have discovered that people in New England enjoy exotic mustard flavors: Champagne mustards, herbed mustards, and even zesty cranberry mustards made from the dried fruit of nearby bogs. A rich maple syrup mustard, incorporating the purest syrup of local sugar maples, is a sure bet, particularly when used to zip up a batch of baked beans.

Cranberry Honey Mustard

¼ cup yellow mustard seeds
1½ cups cider vinegar
1¼ cups dried cranberries (available in health-food stores or the bulk-food section of a well-stocked supermarket)
3 tablespoons honey
1 teaspoon salt

As the dried cranberries soak with the mustard and vinegar, their bright red color leaches out into the vinegar. The resulting mustard is a pretty, cranberry-tinted pink.

In a nonaluminum pot or jar, combine the mustard seeds, vinegar, and cranberries; cover and soak for 48 hours, adding additional vinegar if necessary to maintain enough liquid to cover the seeds.

Scrape the soaked seed-and-cranberry mixture into a food processor and process until the mixture turns from liquid and seeds to a creamy mixture flecked with seeds and bits of cranberry. The process takes at least 3 to 4 minutes, so be patient. You may need to add additional vinegar as necessary to create a nice creamy mustard; keep in mind that it will thicken slightly upon standing. After about one week of aging, the cranberry flavor seems to settle into this mustard and make it all the better, but it is perfectly good immediately.

Makes 3⅓ cups.

American Mustards
135

Whole-Grain Mustard with Malt Vinegar

⅔ cup yellow mustard seeds
½ cup brown mustard seeds
1½ cups malt vinegar
2 cloves garlic, minced
2 teaspoons salt
1 teaspoon sugar
1 teaspoon turmeric

The malt vinegar contributes a bit of sweetness to this condiment, but it is still, basically, a hot and rugged mustard.

In a nonaluminum pot or jar, combine the mustard seeds, vinegar, and garlic; cover and soak for 48 hours, adding additional vinegar if necessary to maintain enough liquid to cover the seeds.

Scrape the soaked seeds into a food processor. Add the salt, sugar, and turmeric and process until the mustard turns from liquid and seeds to a creamy mixture flecked with seeds. This takes 3 to 4 minutes. Add additional vinegar as necessary to create a nice creamy mustard; keep in mind that it will thicken slightly upon standing. This mustard benefits from 2 to 3 weeks of aging.

Makes about 2¼ cups.

New England Maple Syrup Mustard

⅔ cup yellow mustard seeds
½ cup brown mustard seeds
1½ cups malt vinegar
¼ cup pure maple syrup
2 teaspoons salt
About 1½ teaspoons pure maple
   extract

Blend this mustard with a bit of brown sugar and spread it on your next ham during baking. A lovely, zesty-sweet glaze will be your reward.

In a nonaluminum pot or jar, combine the mustard seeds and vinegar; cover and soak for 48 hours, adding additional vinegar if necessary to maintain enough liquid to cover the seeds.

Scrape the soaked seeds into a food processor. Add the maple syrup and salt and process until the mustard turns from liquid and seeds to a creamy mixture flecked with seeds. This takes 3 to 4 minutes. Add additional vinegar as necessary to create a nice creamy mustard; keep in mind that it will thicken slightly upon standing. Stir in the maple extract to taste. This mustard can be consumed immediately.

Makes about 2¼ cups.

Carrots in Sugar and Maple Syrup Mustard Glaze

2 pounds carrots, peeled and
   julienned
⅓ cup butter
⅓ cup sugar
2 teaspoons New England Maple
   Syrup Mustard (see page 136)

These glorious carrots bring a lovely blush of color to a simple poultry dinner. Try not to overcook them while they're in the steamer. After steaming, they should still offer some resistance when pierced with a fork.

Over boiling water, steam the carrots just until barely tender, about 5 minutes. Drain well. In a large skillet, melt the butter over medium to medium-high heat with the sugar and mustard. Add the carrots and continue cooking, stirring often, until the carrots are shiny and glazed. Serve hot.

Makes 8 servings.

Baked Beans in Maple Syrup

For cooks who can't decide whether to add brown sugar or maple syrup to their baked beans (the debate has raged on for decades), why not add both? The addition of the mustard helps balance the sweetness and provides a rich, deep flavor.

To quick-soak the beans, place them in a large kettle with 3 quarts of cold water. Bring to a boil, reduce the heat to medium, and simmer 2 minutes, then remove from the heat and let stand for 1 hour. Alternatively, simply let the beans and water stand overnight.

Drain the beans, cover with fresh water, and cook over medium heat until just barely tender, about 40 minutes. Drain, reserving the cooking liquid. In a 3-quart casserole, combine the beans with the remaining ingredients and 2 cups of the reserved cooking liquid. Bake in a preheated 300°F oven for 3½ to 4 hours, until the beans are very soft, adding additional reserved liquid as needed to keep the beans moist.

Makes 8 servings.

1½ pounds dried navy beans, picked over, rinsed, and drained
¼ pound cubed salt pork or diced bacon
1 cup chopped yellow onion
½ cup firmly packed light brown sugar
½ cup pure maple syrup
1 tablespoon New England Maple Syrup Mustard (see page 136)
½ teaspoon salt

Roast Turkey Breast with Cranberry Mustard Glaze

1 boneless turkey breast, about 3½ to 4 pounds

2 tablespoons Cranberry Honey Mustard (see page 134)

1 tablespoon butter, at room temperature

1 tablespoon firmly packed light brown sugar

The slow-roasting technique produces a succulently moist piece of meat.

Place the turkey breast in a large, shallow roasting pan. Combine the mustard, butter, and brown sugar and spread this mixture over the entire turkey breast.

Roast the turkey in a preheated 225°F oven until a meat thermometer registers 150°F, about 2½ to 3 hours. Remove the turkey from the oven and let it rest on the counter for 20 minutes before slicing to allow the juices to settle.

Makes 6 to 8 servings.

THE MIDWEST

By 1830, one of the most popular destinations for emigrating Germans was the American Midwest. Naturally, such a large concentration of Germans couldn't help but have a major impact on the developing cuisine of the region. Hence, the Midwest palate is considered traditional when it comes to mustard preferences. Indeed, midwesterners do love their horseradish, which is commonly incorporated into a German-Polish-style mustard with lots of seeds and a rich, vinegary flavor.

German-Style Whole-Grain Mustard with Horseradish

The ultimate sausage and hamburger mustard.

In a nonaluminum pot or jar, combine the mustard seeds, vinegar, ale, garlic, and Worcestershire sauce; cover and soak for 48 hours, adding additional vinegar and ale (in equal amounts) if necessary to maintain enough liquid to cover the seeds.

Scrape the soaked seeds into a food processor. Add the remaining ingredients and process until the mustard turns from liquid and seeds to a coarse-grained but creamy mixture flecked with seeds. This takes 2 to 3 minutes. Add additional vinegar and ale (in equal amounts) as necessary to create a nice creamy mustard; keep in mind that it will thicken slightly upon standing.

Makes about 2¾ cups.

⅔ cup yellow mustard seeds
½ cup brown mustard seeds
¾ cup cider vinegar
¾ cup dark ale
3 cloves garlic, minced
1 teaspoon Worcestershire sauce
1 to 2 tablespoons prepared horse-
    radish
1 tablespoon sugar
2 teaspoons salt
2 teaspoons ground allspice
1 teaspoon ground nutmeg
½ teaspoon turmeric

A Reuben Sandwich

1 cup mayonnaise
¼ cup German-Style Whole-Grain
  Mustard with Horseradish (see
  page 141)
12 slices pumpernickel or rye bread
½ pound thinly sliced corned beef
2 cups sauerkraut, rinsed and well
  drained
6 slices Swiss cheese
Butter or margarine

Supposedly, a restaurant cook from Omaha, Nebraska, won the National Sandwich Idea Contest in 1956 with his creation of the Reuben. It didn't take long for the entire country to embrace this stunning combination of cheese, corned beef, and sauerkraut. In no time at all, multiple variations appeared. Here's another one to add to the list.

Combine the mayonnaise and mustard. Spread half of the bread slices with the mayonnaise mixture, then layer on the corned beef, sauerkraut, and cheese. Place the remaining bread slices on top of the cheese. On a large griddle, or in two batches in a heavy skillet, melt the butter over medium heat. Add the sandwiches and grill both sides until they are golden and the cheese has melted.

Makes 6 sandwiches.

Genuine, Honest-to-Goodness, Down-Home Hamburger

The title says it all. This is a meal made with love and care. Don't overlook the homemade relish. Since it's almost always better than anything purchased in the supermarket, your fellow diners will appreciate your attention to such a "gourmet" detail.

Combine the ground sirloin with the minced onion, Worcestershire, mustard, salt, and pepper. Gently shape the mixture into 4 patties. Melt the butter in a skillet over medium-high heat. Add the patties, then reduce the heat to medium and cook to desired level of doneness, about 4 minutes for rare, 6 minutes for medium, and 7 or 8 for well done, turning once after the bottom sides are browned. When the patties are almost cooked, place a slice of cheese on each to melt.

Serve the hamburgers on the prepared buns, passing the Bermuda onion and additional condiments.

Makes 4 servings.

1½ *pounds sirloin, ground (pick out a nicely marbled slab of sirloin in the meat case and have your butcher grind it for you; it will be tender and juicy)*

½ *cup finely minced onion*

1 *tablespoon Worcestershire sauce*

2 *teaspoons German-Style Whole-Grain Mustard with Horseradish (see page 141)*

1 *teaspoon salt*

Freshly ground black pepper to taste

About 2 tablespoons butter

4 *thick slices medium or sharp cheddar cheese*

4 *bakery-fresh fine-quality hamburger buns, toasted*

4 *thick slices Bermuda onion*

Additional condiments: mayonnaise, homemade relish, ketchup, tomatoes, lettuce

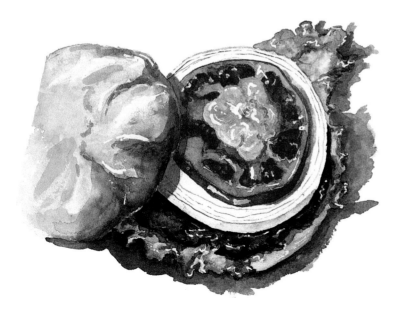

Steamed Cabbage Wedges with Horseradish Mustard Sauce

1 head green cabbage

¼ cup sour cream

¼ cup mayonnaise

2 tablespoons German-Style Whole-
Grain Mustard with Horseradish
(see page 141)

2 tablespoons freshly grated Parmesan cheese

2 teaspoons white wine vinegar

If you're in a hurry, skip the steaming process and simply cut the cabbage into wedges or thick slices and serve in its raw state with the chilled sauce. Most kids (and adults too!) love it.

Cut the cabbage in half, through the core, then cut each half into thirds so you have six wedges (do not core the cabbage). In order to maintain a nice shape to each wedge, run a toothpick through the coreless end of each one. Place the wedges on a steamer rack, cover, and steam over boiling water just until the cabbage becomes tender but still retains some of its crispness, about 8 minutes.

Meanwhile, combine the sour cream, mayonnaise, mustard, Parmesan, and vinegar (this may be prepared up to 48 hours ahead; refrigerate until needed). To serve, arrange the steamed cabbage on a platter. Pass the sauce separately.

Makes 6 servings.

Variation: If you would like a more colorful dish, use red cabbage. When steaming, you must add vinegar to the steaming water (¼ cup of cider vinegar per 1 cup of water) to retain the beautiful red color in the cabbage.

Chapter Six

The Gift of Mustard

When it comes to packaging your homemade mustards, presentation makes all the difference. But that doesn't necessarily mean gargantuan amounts of time spent fussing with glue or needlepoint lid covers. I'm thinking more along the lines of simple bows, elegant jar garnishes that are nothing more than bouquets of dried herbs or flowers, and, perhaps, a collection of stunner jars.

It will help if you start accumulating the appropriate containers for mustard, be they funky stoneware pots or Waterford crystal jam jars. Imported crystal aside, this needn't be an expensive proposition. A walk down any aisle of your grocery store will reveal endless shapes, sizes, and colors of glass jars containing such everyday items as jam, relish, and olives. Once those jars have fulfilled their original purpose in your kitchen, give them a second life as mustard keepers.

Jars

Dedicated mustard makers will have a box in the attic or garage labeled "JARS," in which they can squirrel away any appropriate glass container that comes their way. What constitutes an appropriate mustard jar? Big jars and little jars. Jars with bright red lids and jars with sophisticated black lids. Tall, slender jars and short, fat jars. Antique canning jars with wire bails and glass lids. Collect them all, so that when you make a particular style of mustard you'll have an appropriately styled jar in which to store it.

To get your collection started, consider browsing through second-hand stores and flea markets. They've usually got generous supplies of unusually shaped jars and crocks for five or ten cents apiece. While there, you may also encounter a delightful one-of-a-kind silver spoon to tie to the neck of a mustard gift.

I like to have an especially large assortment of four-ounce jars so I can assemble mustard sampler baskets containing three or four different mustards. Your most convenient source for this size jar will be shops specializing in bulk herbs and spices, but if you want to obtain a large number, the cost will be prohibitive. Better to purchase directly from food manufacturers; check a nearby city for possible sources.

Ideally, the lids on your jar collection should be free of writing, but you can always fix that with a little paint job—as long as you're careful to keep the paint on the outside and away from the rim.

Other Container Ideas

If you want to go for something fancier than jars, you could pack your mustard gift in a lovely porcelain crock or honey pot. Anchor the lid with tape; then, for added insurance against tipping, wrap a square of clear, food-grade cellophane around the entire container, gathering and pleating it at the top, and secure it with a bit of ribbon.

Or, pack the mustard in a plain glass jar, then nestle the jar into a small, lovely bowl that the recipient could use to serve the mustard in. Don't forget to tuck in a uniquely shaped spoon.

Jar Garnishes

If you're handy with ribbons and dried flowers, your mustard could benefit from a lovely miniature bouquet. Carry the theme of the mustard through to the dried arrangement: a mustard with chiles in it, for example, would have a dried chile pepper attached with ribbons to the bouquet; an herbed Dijon bouquet would incorporate dried sprigs of whatever herbs are in the mustard.

For additional ideas on how to put together your bouquets and jar garnishes, drop by a local craft shop. With so many different kinds of paper, ribbon, cellophane, and fabric available these days, your decorated jars can become unique indeed.

What about Labels?

Since there are so many beautiful commercially printed labels available, you don't have to consider this aspect of jar decor unless you're striving for something truly unique. But don't overlook the charm of handmade labels. You needn't be artistic if you can wield a pair of scissors. By clipping out beautiful pictures from magazines and gluing them into a decoupage of colors and images (leave a center portion open so you can write the name of the mustard there), your labels will be one of a kind. Likewise, you could turn your children loose with a box of colored markers and plain white labels. If you aren't working with paper that has an adhesive backing of some sort, I recommend attaching the finished labels to the jars with a spray adhesive. This type of product is less likely than liquid glues and rubber cements to produce air bubbles and will also create a firmer bond between the label and the jar.

Rubber stamps and stencils are also a fast and colorful way to create a batch of labels. Again, by roaming through a well-stocked craft store, you're bound to be inspired by the sheer number of choices available in stamps and stencils.

MUSTARD GIFT BASKETS

Gift baskets are fun to put together because you can match the contents to the interests of the recipient. Start with an appropriate-size basket or gaily decorated box and fill it with at least three different mustards. From there, tailor the basket to the personality, life-style, cooking style, or hobby of the person you're giving it to. Such as:

The Mustard Cook's Basket. For the mustard gourmet wanna-be, provide all the essentials for designer mustard making: a copy of *The Mustard Book*, at least one pound of yellow mustard seeds and half a pound of brown, perhaps a selection of vinegars (rice, balsamic, and wine vinegars would be a nice combination), a collection of four-ounce glass jars (you can usually purchase unused ones at shops specializing in bulk herbs and spices, or, for less money, from a nearby food manufacturer), some jar labels, and, if there's room, a couple of quart-size jars for soaking the seeds.

Fast-Track Basket. For people living in the fast lane, at-home meals are affairs where speed of preparation is a top priority. So fill the basket with a variety of handy food items that can help them throw together a meal in minutes: the mustards, of course, which can be whisked into sauces and vinaigrettes for speedy cooking; jars of mixed seasonings and seasoned salts; fresh pasta and jars of good-quality pasta sauces (well-stocked delicatessens and specialty-food shops always have these on hand); marinated artichoke hearts; and instant soups.

High-Sierra Basket. Pack a high-country picnic with a few appropriate mustards, a crusty loaf of French bread or baguette, a jar of pickles, dry salami, a bottle of red wine (an Oregon Pinot Noir or California Cabernet would be lovely; don't forget the corkscrew!), a package of attractive paper napkins, two plastic wine glasses, and one of those disposable cameras (the kind you use once and then send off to be developed, camera and all).

Basket for the Shore. Tucked into the folds of a beach towel-lined basket you could pack several jars of mustard, a variety of cheeses that complement the mustards, some smoked salmon, whole-grain crackers, a dry white wine, sun visors, and sunscreen.

Fireside Basket. For a wedding shower, anniversary, or "just because" gift promoting a romantic evening in front of the fire, include a few mustards, a bit of pâté (fine-quality ones are available in tins, but if the recipient can refrigerate it as soon as you've handed the basket over, consider a half pound of fresh pâté), a bottle of sparkling wine or Champagne, a small book of romantic verse, and a tape or compact disc of soft (or otherwise romantic) background music.

Sources

For purchasing your whole mustard seeds and powders, keep in mind that you should locate a store that sells them in bulk form. Those tiny tins from the spice aisle in your supermarket cost a fortune. Your most likely sources include health-food stores, food co-ops, feed-and-seed stores, ethnic-food stores, or some particularly well-stocked supermarkets with bulk-food sections. If you locate whole seeds in a gourmet food store, the price may be higher than from these other sources.

If all else fails, you may have to fall back on mail order to obtain your mustard-making materials. The following list will come in handy in that case. Also included in this listing are a few other mustard-related contacts you just may find to be of interest.

The Herb and Spice Collection
P.O. Box 118
Norway, IA 52318
(800) 786-1388

Mustard seeds, mustard powder, beet powder (for coloring raspberry mustard or other fruit mustards). Catalog, $2 (refundable with first order).

Hilltop Herb Farm, Inc.
P.O. Box 325
Romayor, TX 77368
(713) 592-5859

Mustard seeds and mustard powder. Catalog, $2 (refundable with first order).

Mount Horeb Mustard Museum
109 East Main Street
P.O. Box 72
Mount Horeb, WI 53572
(608) 437-3986

A museum completely dedicated to mustard—in Wisconsin? You bet. Barry Levenson is founder and curator of this unique bit of mustard mania. Mustard seeds and powders are available in his retail outlet, or by mail order; Barry also claims to have the largest collection of different prepared mustards for sale (170 and counting) and on exhibit in the museum (1,373 varieties from all corners of the globe, and growing). If you would like information on receiving *The Proper Mustard*, an informative and highly entertaining mustard-dedicated newsletter, write or give Barry a call.

Nichols Garden Nursery
1190 North Pacific Highway
Albany, OR 97321
(503) 928-9280

Mustard seeds, mustard powder, beet powder (for coloring raspberry mustard or other fruit mustards). Free catalog.

Nature's Herb Company
1010 46th Street
Emeryville, CA 94608
(510) 601-0700

Mustard seeds and mustard powder. Catalog, 50 cents.

Tatra Herb Company
222 Grove Street
P.O. Box 60
Morrisville, PA 19067
(215) 295-5476

Mustard seeds and mustard powder. Free catalog.

Williams-Sonoma
P.O. Box 7456
San Francisco, CA 94120-7456
(800) 541-2233

This marvelous catalog for serious and recreational cooks contains Boyajian's wonderful flavored oils (orange oil, garlic oil, chili oil, and mustard oil) and designer sausages, including chicken and apple, chicken and turkey, turkey-herb, Cajun andouille, and whiskey-fennel-pork. Free catalog.

Index